"This excellent book is a fresh, ⟨
up the importance, vitality, and

—w. Kobert Gouney, chairman, ⟨g

"Protestant worship can appear to be boring. The remedy for some is to add beauty and grandeur, and for others, excitement. The Reformers understood that biblical worship needed spice but that such pizzazz came not from externals or style but from Scripture, faith, and a right understanding of what transpires when God's people meet in His name on the Lord's Day. Jonathan Cruse uses the teaching of Scripture and the wisdom of Reformed theologians to remind Protestants how extraordinary their simple worship is."
—D. G. Hart, associate professor of history, Hillsdale College

"As responsibility for the faithful transmission of Reformed ministry and worship passes from one generation to the next, Jonathan Cruse has shown himself willing and able to take up the mantle. He presents the old strengths of God-centered, gospel-structured, Spirit-dependent, word-filled, and Bible-regulated worship with a fresh voice, conveying to this generation the genius of worship that is Reformed 'according to Scripture.'"
—Terry L. Johnson, senior minister, Independent
Presbyterian Church, Savannah, Georgia

"I am amazed at how much solid material Jonathan Cruse has managed to pack into these few pages of *What Happens When We Worship*! Each aspect I think of on this vital subject is addressed succinctly and with biblical fidelity. I love the questions for further discussion. They turn you from a mere intellectual student into a fellow participant in a quest for authentic, God-glorifying worship. Read this book, and you will increasingly put mind, heart, and soul into your worship with renewed enthusiasm."
—Conrad Mbewe, pastor, Kabwata Baptist Church, Lusaka, Zambia

"Jonathan Cruse gives us a fresh work that can help unite several generations in a recovery of regularly anticipating heaven on earth. This work is accessible to all—biblically informed, practically oriented, and well presented. I am happy to commend it and especially recommend the final sections on worship, rightly offered. We can only hope that the coming generation will heed this new and young voice—rooted in much more than his own limited experience."
—David W. Hall, senior pastor, Midway Presbyterian
Church, Powder Springs, Georgia

"When we come together to worship, we do so as members of Christ's mystical body, drawing near to the Father in the Son by the Spirit, knowing that the triune God draws near to us and draws us up into the heavenlies where we worship Him in spirit and truth. This sentence describes the most astounding reality possible, one that lies beyond our imagining, eclipsing every earthly glory and imbuing worshipers with the glory of the world to come, a reality that is joy unspeakable. Jonathan Landry Cruse seeks to impart something of that inexpressible glory in this well-written and well-argued gem that helps us to understand the true experience of worship, an experience transcending all lesser views of worship, whether those stressing entertainment or an overstuffed liturgy or anything that falls short of the glory of biblical new covenant worship. Read this to understand better this dynamic that occurs in Reformed worship or to introduce someone who longs for such but has never known it. Cruse, an accomplished musician and OPC pastor, beautifully lays out the heart of such worship before us. Let all come and partake freely of these divine waters that quench the inner thirst and never run dry."

—Alan D. Strange, professor of church history, Mid-America Reformed Seminary

"Jonathan Cruse's must-read, page-turning book on worship is masterful both in explaining what is really going on when we worship our holy and gracious triune God corporately as well as why and how we ought to engage with each part of a biblically grounded and biblically marinated worship service. One doesn't need to wholeheartedly amen every detail this innovative book offers to have a profound appreciation for the way the author biblically and practically shows the place of priority that public worship ought to have in the life of every Christian. I wondered as I read this convicting and yet exhilarating book: If true believers embrace this high and moving view of worship, would the church soon see much greater days of repentance, reformation, and revival? May God forgive us for our paltry and backsliding view of worship and fill us with Himself and His glory and beauty (Ps. 27:4) as we strive to worship Him in Spirit and truth."

—Joel R. Beeke president, Puritan Reformed Theological Seminary; and pastor, Heritage Reformed Congregation, Grand Rapids, Michigan

"Jonathan Cruse has written a helpful, popular-level guide to corporate worship, which can only serve to enrich the worship of the Christian believer each Lord's Day and, in turn, the church as a whole. This is a book every minister should encourage every member to read. It will help us all to worship through new eyes, appreciating more deeply why we do what we do when we gather together as Christ's church."

—Jonny Gibson, associate professor of Old Testament, Westminster Theological Seminary, Philadelphia

What Happens When We
WORSHIP

What Happens When We
WORSHIP

Jonathan Landry Cruse

Reformation Heritage Books
Grand Rapids, Michigan

Reformation Heritage Books
2965 Leonard St. NE
Grand Rapids, MI 49525
616-977-0889
orders@heritagebooks.org
www.heritagebooks.org

Printed in the United States of America
20 21 22 23 24 25/10 9 8 7 6 5 4 3 2 1

Library of Congress Cataloging-in-Publication Data

Names: Cruse, Jonathan Landry, author.
Title: What happens when we worship / Jonathan Landry Cruse.
Description: Grand Rapids, Michigan : Reformation Heritage Books, [2020] | Includes bibliographical references.
Identifiers: LCCN 2020037446 (print) | LCCN 2020037447 (ebook) | ISBN 9781601788160 (paperback) | ISBN 9781601788177 (epub)
Subjects: LCSH: Worship.
Classification: LCC BV10.3 .C78 2020 (print) | LCC BV10.3 (ebook) | DDC 264—dc23
LC record available at https://lccn.loc.gov/2020037446
LC ebook record available at https://lccn.loc.gov/2020037447

For additional Reformed literature, request a free book list from Reformation Heritage Books at the above regular or email address.

To my parents,
with warmest love and unspeakable gratitude

And "to him who loves us and has freed us from our sins
by his blood and made us a kingdom, priests to his God
and Father, to him be glory and dominion forever
and ever." (Rev. 1:5–6 ESV)

Contents

Foreword

My parents enjoyed telling about the first time they visited a Reformed church. Late for church, they decided to walk across the street to a Dutch Reformed congregation. "What was it like?" They explained the liturgy in detail, with its back-and-forth movement between God's speech and the congregation's response, including corporate confession of sin and declaration of pardon, the Apostles' Creed, and the Lord's Prayer. "It seemed Catholic," they said. "We didn't know anything but our own church background"—which definitely was not *that*.

Walking into a traditional Reformed or Presbyterian service, one might at first blush feel a little out of place. Hopefully, there are at least warm greetings from members before and after, maybe even an offer of hospitality to someone's home, but the service itself can feel like you're crashing someone else's family reunion.

Reformed worship is certainly not Roman Catholic or high church, but it is also quite different from most evangelical settings. Precisely because it is a family gathering of those who are united in Christ by common Christian beliefs and practices but also with distinct inflections, it's the type of thing that grows on you. There is a depth to the fellowship in common baptism, prayer, praise, the hearing of the word (often lengthy sections) read and preached, and the Lord's Supper. It takes a while, but there is a reason for things. It isn't just tradition, but a long practice that is at least supposed to be grounded thoroughly in Scripture.

Many Reformed and Presbyterian churches today happily cast off what they consider the chains of a scripturally regulated gathering of God's people, embracing either more high-church or contemporary worship. Bored with the simplicity of Reformed worship, many find in other churches more exciting features. Some prefer to be engulfed in the sights and sounds of mystery, while others want to be enveloped in the more familiar sights and sounds of popular culture. But we have to stop and ask ourselves, "What happens in worship?"

The so-called worship wars—whether we have an organ and choir or a praise band—are distracting us from asking this deeper question. Jonathan Cruse has already given a taste of what he is up to with his title. Indeed, what happens?

The answer for many churchgoers, whether high church or low, is mainly about what *we* do. We go to church to praise the Lord, for example. Or we go to church to fellowship. In our most honest moments, we might say that we go to church because we're commanded to—it's a duty, a habit. According to Roman Catholic teaching, the liturgy is "the work of the people"; although more involved in the service since Vatican II, the people are still largely spectators until, with the priest and the whole church, they offer the sacrifice of the Mass. In contemporary evangelical settings, the professionals on the stage are often just as prominent. In any case, the idea across the spectrum seems to be that we are the active party. It is our fervor and zeal or our correct performance of ritual that brings God down to us.

More important than any other distinctive of Reformed worship is that we come primarily not to serve but to be served by God the Father, in His Son, through the power of the Spirit working through His word. Just as He did in John 13, Jesus comes to wash His disciples' feet. He comes to give us a kingdom, to make us part of His kingdom. He announces full pardon and justification by grace alone simply on the basis of what He has done. He is present in the word—preached, sung, read, and given in baptism and the Supper. As we are told by the apostle Paul in Romans 10, we do not have to climb up to heaven to bring Him down or descend into the depths to somehow make Him alive and present among us. "But what does it say? 'The word is near you, in your mouth and in your heart' (that is, the word of faith that we proclaim)" (v. 8 ESV). We place so much emphasis on the word because it is through the gospel that the Spirit creates and sustains the faith of longtime believers and outsiders alike. Every service should be evangelistic!

There is definitely an important place for praise, but, as in the Psalms—the inspired book of praise—God's work has to be set before us before we have anything for which to praise Him. I always find it interesting when I hear the musical part of the service referred to as the "worship time." In many contexts, the time devoted to the reading and exposition of Scripture as well as common confession and prayer pale in comparison to the often individualistic self-expression of singing along with the musicians. We sing not merely to express our piety but, again, to receive: "Let the word of Christ dwell in you richly, teaching and admonishing one another in all wisdom, singing psalms and hymns and spiritual songs, with thankfulness in your hearts to God" (Col. 3:16 ESV). Interestingly, we are not just expressing our feelings to God but are "addressing one another in psalms and hymns and spiritual songs, singing and making melody to the Lord with [our] heart" (Eph. 5:19 ESV). Reformed Christians have always cherished singing the Psalms especially because there is a song for every occasion and emotion. It's not all joyful praise. There are also agonizing lament, honest questioning, and spiritual depression. Our Christian experience is a mixed bag. It is a real relationship with the Father in Christ, and so we should be able to relate honestly with God together and to have our eyes lifted up together in hope by His promises.

There is also an important place for fellowship. After all, each local church is an expression of the one body of Christ. Yet here too, there can be no church at all without the word—not only preached but read and prayed and sung and received in the two sacraments appointed by Christ. Our fellowship is not generated by shared cultural influences or generational, ethnic, socioeconomic, or political affinity; not by the sort of music we like (opera versus rock concert), but by "one Lord, one faith, one baptism" (Eph. 4:5).

There is an important place for duty—even good habits. Sometimes we do not feel like going to church, but if mere obligation gets us to where the gifts are, we return home the richer. Yet mere duty in the long run, without the gospel, is vain and superstitious.

There are many important biblical teachings shaping Reformed worship that this book will explain. The most important thing, however, is that it's not about us but for us. We come to church not even primarily to worship but to receive once again that life-sustaining Bread of Life in the variety of ways His word comes to us. We come not to do something again, but to have something done to us again; not to join various causes and kingdoms in this age, but because Christ has "*made* [us] a kingdom and priests to our God" who are justified, are being sanctified, "and they shall reign on the earth" (Rev. 5:10 ESV, emphasis added).

What happens in worship? God is at work, and the best thing we can do is receive it. I've known Jonathan Cruse for many years now and have enormous respect for his gifts not only in theology but in music. This book will broaden and deepen your vision while narrowing it on "the Author and Finisher of our faith." *Please* read, mark, and inwardly digest the teaching in this important book.

—Michael Horton
J. Gresham Machen Professor of
Systematic Theology and Apologetics
Westminster Seminary California

Acknowledgments

My interest in all things related to worship began in earnest in my college years, when, in God's providence, I became close friends with several different church musicians. The world of corporate worship was open to me through the beautiful doors of corporate praise. These friends and mentors got me thinking about excellence in worship as a whole, something I had given far too little thought to before. For that, I am grateful to Paul, Tim, and Jared.

In terms of this particular manuscript, thanks is due to my dear friends Bob and Mary Jackson, who carefully combed through my many mistakes, offered extraordinary insight and helpful suggestions, and have made this a much stronger work.

I am indebted to the expert critique, comments, and encouragement offered by Glen Clary, Jonny Gibson, Darryl Hart, Terry Johnson, and Alan Strange. Go read all of their work on worship. Likewise, I am extremely humbled by the edifying foreword by Michael Horton, whose work on this subject has had a deep influence in my life. My colleagues Luke Sayers and Jeff Wilson were exceptional conversation partners throughout the project, and Linda and Bob Jones helped in ways that only they can.

The session of Community Presbyterian Church, my co-laborers in Christ and fathers in the faith, have been a constant support. In particular, Perry Westerman read through an early draft and offered helpful corrections. The majority of this material began as a Sunday school course for the members of Community. The eagerness of our congregation to learn about this important topic brought (and still brings) fuel for me in my ministry. Thank you, dear saints!

Thanks are due to the RHB team, who have been so wonderful to work with yet again. Thank you to Joel, David, Steve, and Annette! And especially to Jay, who championed this project from the very beginning. Thank you to my wife, Kerri Ann, for always sharing in my excitement about writing projects. I don't know where I would be without her constant encouragement.

Finally, I offer my deepest gratitude to my parents. Dad and Mom: you cultivated an atmosphere of eager anticipation every week as we would get ready for church. Even through difficult days in the lives of our various congregations, worship was a priority—and a joyful one at that. Sunday mornings are some of my fondest memories of growing up in the yellow house on Walnut Street. To you both I dedicate this book.

Chapter 1

What Happens When We Worship?

The truly penitent man glories in the supernatural, for he knows that nothing natural would meet his need.
— J. Gresham Machen

Worship is a supernatural event. Have you ever considered that?

It's an obvious statement, really. An event in which we interact with a supernatural being must, by definition, be supernatural. Then why is it that we so often approach worship with a sense of boredom instead of astonishment, with yawns instead of awe, with resentment instead of reverence? Why is it that rather than seeing worship as a supernatural event, we clump it in with the other mundane things we have to get done during the week? Going to church gets the same checkmark on the to-do list as going to the grocery store or doing homework.

If I were to ask you, What happens when you go to church?—that is, what goes on during the actual worship service—how would you answer? Some people might answer, "Well, there's some preaching, a little praying, and a lot of singing." Others may say, "We read our Bibles, watch a presentation from the youth group, stand up at one point and shake everyone's hand," and so on. But that's not what I mean. Those answers tell me the various elements that make up the service. My question is one that seeks to go beyond that. What are these elements for? What are they accomplishing? What *happens* when we worship?

This book is written from a simple but important premise: something *is happening* when we worship. Something happens *to* us, something happens *between* us and the people we worship with, and, most importantly, something happens *between us and God*.

Many people hold to a "spectator" approach to worship: church is somewhere you go to watch something. You might stand up here or there and recite a line or two printed in the bulletin or shown on the big screen; in that sense you are participating, but by and large the event is something to watch. This makes going to worship not much different from going to the movies or to a football game. Others hold to a "club" approach: church is somewhere you go to hang around with like-minded people and do projects together. From this perspective, what goes on in church is not different from what goes on at 4H, the Girl Scouts, or your local book club.

But what goes on in the church's worship *is* different from these things! Going to worship is different from going to the cinema or the stadium, and it's different from attending a meeting of a local social club because worship—real, true, faithful worship—is supernatural. The God of the universe appears and meets with His people, and by His sovereign and gracious power He changes them. It's astounding! It's unlike anything this world could ever offer. And yet how easy it is to forget that something as spectacular as this is happening when we come to church.

The Church Is a Bore, but She Is Our Mother

Astounding and *spectacular* are perhaps not the first adjectives most people would use to describe the average church-going experience, especially in the traditionally Reformed genre from which this book is written. Along with *astounding* and *spectacular* you could also strike *thrilling, exciting,* and any other word that even hints at the idea that worship could capture affections and attentions. Instead, many people would charge worship with being boring, dull, dry, and tedious. And even if some of us haven't said it out loud, most of us have thought it at one point.

Some Christians think boredom in worship is a badge of honor. In an effort to ensure that the church remains distinct from the world, they have mistakenly presumed that God actually intends our services to be insipid. They believe the monotony to be a sign of sincere worship. Anything that might stir the emotions must be from Satan. There are still others who, though they may not enjoy that church is boring, have errantly concluded that this must be the way it is. They have resigned themselves to slugging through the humdrum of Sunday out of obligation (whether to God, family, or friends) but are dreaming of something better that must be out there for them—think forlorn Belle from *Beauty and the Beast* singing, "There must be more than this provincial life!"

Let's at least admit that at first glance the worship service can seem dull. There's no point arguing that. There is a lot of sitting. There is a lot of listening. There is a lot of patience required. For an active culture with a notoriously short attention span constantly inundated with images, videos, push notifications, and ringers, it is no wonder an hour of concerted stillness seems like a chore.

But just because it seems dull doesn't mean it is dull. It simply means we are not aware of what is happening when we worship. This is why God is not pleased with those who wear the boredom badge with honor or with those who dutifully suffer through the service while secretly wishing church wasn't an obligation. God is not pleased with this because in both cases these people have completely missed out on the marvel of worship. God wants from us nothing less than hearts, souls, and minds that are fully enraptured with the wonder of biblical worship from beginning to end—which is to say, He wants us to be fully enraptured with Him. He wants us thrilled at the thought of coming to church to sing His praise, fellowship with His saints, lift up our prayers to His throne, hear His word, celebrate the sacraments of His covenant, and receive His blessing. Anything else would mean we fail at the great exhortation of Psalm 100:2: "Serve the LORD with gladness."

After an Aesthetic

Sadly, many Christians think that the only way to worship with joy and gladness is through manufactured means. So what have people done to solve this perceived weariness of worship? Generally speaking, when the boredom and dullness of worship become too oppressive, people will turn to one of two alternatives: an aesthetic of entertainment or an aesthetic of mysticism.[1]

---

1. Terry L. Johnson notes something similar using the categories of the "Contemporary Worship Movement" and the "Liturgical Renewal Movement," which cropped

The Entertainment Aesthetic
The first alternative is perhaps the most prevalent today, and that is
the solution proposed by the modern mainstream evangelical church.
These churches generally have a very talented (and/or loud) band leading the singing. Perhaps the music is the bulk of the church's worship
activity. There will be cool graphics and videos projected onto a large
screen to accompany the various portions of the service. The pastor
invariably will be charming and hip, and his messages will be con-
versational and "down-to-earth." The church will provide an array of
programs that will keep your kids busy throughout the week—and even
during the worship service.

Admittedly, this is a bit of a stereotype, but it paints a picture of
what many in mainstream evangelicalism are doing today. They are
pursuing a particular aesthetic in worship, and it really is nothing
other than the aesthetic of entertainment. Many church services will
be barely distinguishable from secular concert venues: dim sanctuary,
impressive stage lighting and props, and loud music. Church becomes
a place where you go to be entertained. A Sunday morning with your
church family ends up looking not all that different from a Saturday
night out with your friends.

The Garden, a progressive United Methodist church in Indianapo-
lis, is an example. The "worship" band generally plays popular secular
music played on many radio stations. The sermons are around fifteen
minutes long and are often interspersed with video clips from famous
movies. On The Garden's website, they boast that their church "suc-
ceeds in blurring the lines between the sacred and secular." The reason?
To get people into church! According to this approach, the sacred is
boring and unappealing, but the secular will draw people in and keep
them in.

Another illustration of this approach comes from a pastor friend
of mine who was driving with his family down south when they
passed a billboard for a local church. There were several photos on the

---

up to fill the void created by a lack of attention to historic Reformed Protestant worship.
*Worshipping with Calvin: Recovering the Historic Ministry and Worship of Reformed Prot-
estantism* (Darlington, England: EP, 2014), 27.

advertisement: a band onstage with lights and fog, children playing games outside, and young couples laughing around the coffee bar. In big, bold letters the caption read: "Church was never meant to be boring."

I couldn't agree more with that statement. Church was never meant to be boring. And, in fact, church isn't boring. But you can see what the caption combined with those images was implying: this particular congregation had recovered 11 a.m. on Sunday from the dungeon of droll. They were saying, "Come worship with us. We have made church exciting! We have made it fun! We have made it entertaining! Don't be bored when you could have a good time enjoying the show we put on for you!" There's a flaw in this thinking, though: that worship is something we have to *make* exciting. No, corporate worship is not boring, and that's not because of anything we do; it's because of God's presence in and among us. No matter our productions or programs, we can't manufacture that kind of supernatural wonder—and we certainly can't top it either.

A more serious flaw with this approach—a fatal flaw, even—is that it wins people to worship with something that will tickle their fancies and yet never save their souls. This approach (sometimes deigned "seeker sensitive") did not just fall out of the sky in the last few decades. The intrusion of entertainment in worship today can trace its roots back to the work of revivalist minister Charles G. Finney (1792–1875). An American Presbyterian minister, Finney became famous for the methods employed at his meetings, later known as the "new measures," which were carefully designed to manipulate an emotional response from the crowd. For Finney, there was a formula that, employed correctly, would guarantee interest in the things of God. He said so himself: "A revival is not a miracle, or dependent on a miracle in any sense. It is a purely philosophic [i.e., scientific] result of the right use of the constituted means."[2] It was this sort of ministry that caused Charles Spurgeon (1834–1892) to remark in the 1800s that "the devil has seldom done a cleverer thing than hinting to the church that part of their mission is to

---

2. As quoted in D. G. Hart and John R. Muether, *Seeking a Better Country: 300 Years of American Presbyterianism* (Phillipsburg, N.J.: P&R, 2007), 113.

provide entertainment for the people, with a view to winning them."[3] These words are just as true today.

The Mystical Aesthetic

For some people, a second alternative to enduring the supposed banality of Reformed worship is to join the ranks of more ritualistic and High Church worship services provided by the likes of Eastern Orthodoxy, Roman Catholicism, and Episcopacy. They by and large reject the drum set and light show for the literal smells and bells of these more mystical services. Mystics, narrowly speaking, believe that a person can be caught up into the divine essence by sincere meditation and contemplation, by casting off the trappings of the physical world and being lost in reflection on the spiritual world. I am sure many congregations and congregants are not after anything as ambitious as becoming one with the divine essence (though this is a main tenant in Eastern Orthodox teaching). Many people follow mysticism in the broader sense of the term, hoping for worship to give them an experience and the sense that they are part of something greater and more important than their everyday routine; something more fantastical, something otherworldly—indeed, something supernatural.

My argument in this book is that something supernatural is happening when we worship. This group would agree entirely. But they would say that in their services you can actually *feel* what's happening. It's not the entertainment aesthetic; it's a mystical aesthetic. There is something that seems to be spiritually palpable about incense, chants, and gestures. There has been an increase in the last few decades of Protestants abandoning their tradition for the sake of Roman Catholicism, and pastor and theologian Sam Storms concludes that a major reason is for these aesthetic matters: "Many appeal to the experience of being moved by the architecture of Roman Catholic church structures, the incense, the beauty of liturgy, the mystery, the solemnity, the drama,

3. C. H. Spurgeon, "Feeding Sheep or Amusing Goats," *Reformation and Revival* 2, no. 1 (Winter 1993), Resource Library, The Gospel Coalition, http://resources.thegospel coalition.org/library/feeding-sheep-or-amusing-goats.

the vestments of the clergy, the church calendar, the sense of transcendence, religious symbolism," he writes.[4]

In many cases, this mystical aura is achieved at the price of theology. As an example, take the Roman Catholic doctrine of transubstantiation, which asserts that the bread and wine literally transform into the actual body and blood of Christ. There is something stirring at the thought of being able to tangibly hold Christ, and this is undoubtedly why many people are drawn to this type of worship. But does a biblical and Reformed service offer us anything less? Biblical and Reformed theology states that we are present with Christ through the ministry and mystery of the Holy Spirit for the entirety of the worship service. What, then, would be appealing about a doctrine that gives me Christ for only a few brief seconds in a tiny wafer and a few drops of wine?

Another popular reason Protestants are jumping ship for Rome is because of perceived historical pedigree.[5] Could it be that the Reformation was a rebellion against the true Christian religion and the Roman Catholics are the keepers of the sacred faith once delivered to all the saints? More than that, compared to the splintering of countless denominations in Protestantism, the Roman Catholic Church seems to stand as solid and strong as one of her ancient cathedrals. Stepping into its worship can feel like going back in time. But there are issues with this argument as well. Just because something feels old, and even is old, does not mean it is right. Besides, Reformed Protestantism also boasts an ancient tradition—the whole way back to the apostles. Our worship is a reflection of the devotion of the New Testament church, which "continued steadfastly in the apostles' doctrine and fellowship, in the breaking of bread, and in prayers" (Acts 2:42). All this, mind you, took place in people's homes and not inside breathtaking cathedrals.

Aspects of this mystical approach—the theological considerations of architecture or the concerted effort to use form prayers and other liturgical practices, for example—are by no means inherently wrong

4. Sam Storms, "Another Protestant Converts to Catholicism: Why?," *Enjoying God* (blog), April 3, 2014, https://www.samstorms.org/enjoying-god-blog/post/another-protestant-converts-to-catholicism:-why.

5. For an excellent treatment on this matter, see D. G. Hart, *Still Protesting: Why the Reformation Still Matters* (Grand Rapids: Reformation Heritage Books, 2018).

or unbiblical. But there is a major problem when we think we need to go through these motions to achieve anything meaningful in worship. Again, worship *is* meaningful—not because of what we do but because of what God is doing in and through us by His Spirit.

Awakened to Worship

Many people approach worship as though it were the ecclesiastical equivalent of brussels sprouts, which we all know can be stomached only if they are roasted in oil, tossed in balsamic vinegar and honey, and heavily salted (even better if wrapped in bacon!). But worship is not brussels sprouts. It doesn't need to be dressed up. It is entirely wonderful all on its own. But we can often be blind to that. Even in a church that seeks to worship according to God's prescribed methods in Scripture— in a service where God's Spirit is present and active—the worshipers themselves can be completely unaware of what is going on around them. This means that how a particular congregation approaches the worship service as a corporate entity is not all that matters—how I myself as a Christian individual and son and servant of God approach worship is of crucial significance.

John Antioco would know what I'm talking about. Antioco was the former CEO of Blockbuster, who, back in 2000, passed up the opportunity to buy a fledgling company known as Netflix for only fifty million dollars. You know the rest of the story. Blockbuster is out of business and Netflix is now worth well over thirty billion dollars.[6] Just because Antioco was blind to the potential of Netflix didn't mean it lacked potential. Indeed, his decision cost him the deal of a lifetime. In church we often miss out on a great deal, just as Antioco did. Our vision is clouded to the potential—truly, the power—of what is going on around us in worship. But just because we don't see or sense it doesn't mean it's not there. It just means we need the same thing that Elisha's servant needed: we need God to open our eyes (2 Kings 6:17–20).

---

6. Celena Chong, "Blockbuster's CEO Once Passed Up a Chance to Buy Netflix for Only $50 Million, July 17, 2015, https://www.businessinsider.com/blockbuster-ceo -passed-up-chance-to-buy-netflix-for-50-million-2015-7.

If you are like me, you have grown up in the church—for me it was a Presbyterian and Reformed church, but this could be your experience coming from any ecclesiastical background—and the aspects of worship have become somewhat second nature. They don't require you to give much thought to them. Much like you don't have to think very hard about the route you drive to church week in and week out, you find you do not have to think very hard about what you are doing in church when you actually get there. Almost mechanically your hand is on the songbook as the "amen" is said in the opening prayer. The check goes into the offering plate and you don't even remember writing it. Worship has become a going-through-the-motions exercise. Sadly, this is the case for many Christians today.

This is not a new problem. Puritan Jeremiah Burroughs (1599–1646) had to exhort the people of his day to "learn what it is you do when you come to worship God." He says that if he went from one side of his congregation to the next and asked each person, "Is it your duty to worship God?" they would all answer proudly in the affirmative. Burroughs laments, however, that if he were to go around the sanctuary again and ask, "And what does worship look like exactly? What is it that you do when you worship? What is happening when you worship?" many of those same congregants would be perplexed and speechless.[7]

The Aim of This Book

This book seeks to remedy that ignorance and indifference that have plagued and continue to plague many worshiping Christians. By exposing what's really happening in these moments of corporate worship, I hope to take the rote out of the routine and in its place produce a zeal for God and gratitude to Him for what He does for us in worship. I want to open our eyes—to wake us up—to what is going on (and has *always* been going on) around us every time we gather to worship in Spirit and in truth. Since God is an infinite God, His worship is infinitely interesting. We can never plumb the depths of who He is nor ever exhaust the stores of His goodness, grace, and glory. Worship is

---

7. Jeremiah Burroughs, *Gospel Worship: Worship Worthy of God* (1653; repr., Morgan, Pa.: Soli Deo Gloria, 1990), 35.

the grand exploration and exaltation of who God is. If the moment of worship seems dull to us, the fault lies with us, not with God.

To do this, part 1 will establish some guiding principles about worship, generally speaking. We could consider this a brief biblical theology of worship: tracing what the Scriptures teach us about the nature, purpose, and result of meeting with God as His called and gathered people.

The following chapters in part 2 will unpack what actually happens during each of the major elements of standard Reformed worship. Here we zoom in and carefully walk through each element of the service. For indeed, the entirety of the service is worship! The worship service does not primarily reside in the sermon, nor are we only worshiping when we sing (a misconception not helped by our regular use of *worship* as a synonym for *music*). According to D. A. Carson, "it is folly to think that only part of the 'service' is worship." This kind of understanding of corporate worship is "so bizarre, from a New Testament perspective, as to be embarrassing."[8] Every aspect of the Lord's Day service, from the call to worship to the benediction, is worship, which is why this book on worship will devote some time to every element.

God is doing something to us and for us and through us in each element of the worship service. We will be exploring how God uses things like reading the Bible, singing, preaching, and the Lord's Supper as means to convict us of sin and actually conform us into the people we are meant to be. We will see worship is the place where we undergo a transformation. Who would have thought something as "boring" as church could do something so thrilling? Maybe church isn't boring after all! It's a powerful thing, worship. And it deserves our careful attention. Part 3 will conclude with some observations and tips on how we can best do just that.

A prayer of mine is that this book may also prove useful if you are not a Christian and have very little experience with worship. If you've ever wondered, *What are those people doing every Sunday?* this book will help. The practice of churchgoing can seem bizarre. After all, aren't there better ways to spend a Sunday? (The answer is no.) My prayer

---

8. D. A. Carson, "Worship under the Word," in *Worship by the Book*, ed. D. A. Carson (Grand Rapids: Zondervan, 2002), 47.

is that this book will show you why Christians devote such time and energy to the act of worship and why you should too.

But ultimately I want to recover worship from the doldrums. Let me rephrase that: I want to recover the *perception* of worship as being the doldrums. Worship is never dull, but we are sometimes. Churchgoing is monotonous and mundane only because our eyes are blinded to the supernatural wonder that is taking place all around us. The reality is that worship is an exhilarating experience. So we don't need smoke machines, more lights, dramatic presentations, louder music, mystical theology, or entertaining speakers to make worship exciting. We simply need to understand what's going on in the first place. It doesn't matter if your week is filled with skydiving, speed racing, or whatever your personal taste for adventure might be. No matter what your week looks like, Sunday worship is the highlight. And we're going to see why in this book.

Admittedly, we are just going to be scratching the surface here. There could easily be ten more chapters in this book, and each chapter could easily be ten times longer. But I'm not seeking to present a fully exhaustive treatment on the subject of worship. Rather, this is meant to be an important introduction to, or perhaps a gentle reminder of, the topic. My aim is to whet your appetite when it comes to worship. For indeed it is in corporate worship that we are able to "taste and see that the LORD is good" (Ps. 34:8).

Discussion Questions
1. Why do we so often find church to be boring?

2. In what ways have Christians attempted to manufacture "exciting" worship experiences?

3. Describe the "entertainment aesthetic" and the "mystical aesthetic" approaches to worship.

4. In what ways are these different approaches distinct from one another and in what ways are they similar to one another?

5. How is ignorance a major problem for us when we come to worship?

PART 1:
A (Brief) Theology of Worship

Chapter 2

The Most Important Thing
We Will Ever Do

Man's chief end is to glorify God and enjoy Him forever.
—Westminster Shorter Catechism

Contrary to what we may think and feel, worship is exciting. And worship is important. In fact, w*orship is the most important thing you will ever do.* Period. We can never consider worship too often; we can never study this topic too much. The most important thing you will do every week, no matter what your week looks like, will be to come to worship on Sunday. So to the question, What is happening when we worship? we have our first answer: the most important thing you could ever do is happening!

To some readers this might sound like an audacious and preposterous proposition. How can we make this claim? Certainly there are any number of meaningful things we can do with our time here on earth. Why does this one rise to the top? It's not as simple as pointing to chapter and verse to prove my point, but there are at least two reasons why it should be evident that worship is what matters most.

Internal Design
First is the simple fact that we were created to worship. This was God's purpose for us from the very beginning. And though the fall messed up a lot of things about what it means to be a true human, one thing could not be eradicated completely: our innate desire to worship. It's natural to us. It's built into who we are. It's what I'm calling the argument from *internal design.* Our hearts were made to yearn for, desire after, and

offer worship to God (see Psalms 63 and 84). The Westminster divines, a group of European theologians in the seventeenth century who composed the Westminster Confession of Faith (WCF) and the Westminster Larger (WLC) and Shorter Catechisms (WSC), got it absolutely right when they said that our chief end is to "glorify God and enjoy Him forever."[1] "Chief end" is just another way of saying "design." It's what we were made for.

The Sense of Deity

Human beings were made to know God. God placed in the human soul the ability to know Him and commune with Him, or in other words, worship Him. And this is what Adam and Eve did before the fall: they knew God, and they enjoyed Him. They walked in His presence. They lived with Him. Indeed, Eden was not a luxurious resort secluded from the rest of the world that God created expressly for the two of them to inhabit. Rather, it was His home, His sanctuary—the very first temple. Therefore, as Adam and Eve dwelt in the garden they also dwelt with the Lord.

As we look at the opening chapters of Genesis before the fall, we see that this constant worship in the continual presence of God is what we were made for. In the beginning, when a synapse fired, it did so at the sight of God's splendor. Every heartbeat—that is, every passionate desire—was for Him. Every neurological reception was stuffed with divine majesty. God was everywhere present after all! There was nothing to behold apart from His beauty in creation. And apart from the creation, there was the Creator Himself, who manifested Himself among them and dwelt with them. Since there was no sin to distract them from His splendor and majesty, we could even say that knowing God and worshiping Him were instinctual.

In his *Institutes of the Christian Religion*, renowned Reformer John Calvin makes the similar point that humankind was made to worship:

> There is within the human mind, and indeed by natural instinct, an awareness of divinity. This we take to be beyond controversy. To prevent anyone from taking refuge in the pretense of ignorance,

---

1. WSC 1.

God himself has implanted in all men a certain understanding of his divine majesty.... Yet there is, as the eminent pagan says, no nation so barbarous, no people so savage, that they have not a deep-seated conviction that there is a God. And they who in other aspects of life seem least to differ from brutes still continue to retain some seed of religion. So deeply does the common conception occupy the minds of all, so tenaciously does it inhere in the hearts of all! Therefore, since from the beginning of the world there has been no region, no city, in short, no household, that could do without religion, there lies in this a tacit confession of a sense of deity inscribed in the hearts of all.[2]

In theology, this sense of deity is known as the *sensus divinitas,* and we all have it. We all have something inside of us that tells us there is Something Greater out there, and we owe Him our worship. Cliché as it may sound (and it is cliché), we all have a God-shaped hole in our hearts. And the only way it can be filled is through worship. The problem is that we so often try to fill up that emptiness with the wrong kind of worship.

This was the problem at the very beginning, wasn't it? Adam and Eve had the *sensus divinitas*; they were made to know that there was Something Greater out there. They also knew what (or better who) that Something Greater was. They knew their Maker, and they knew they were called to worship Him. What plunged humanity into the curse of sin was an act of misplaced worship. Eve sought her own glory rather than God's. But as Calvin hints in the above quote, even the fall could not take away the pull of religion. Even the fall could not eradicate our internal design, which is to be worshipers. What has changed is *what* we desire to worship, but the desire itself is still there. And it always will be.

Paul writes about this in Romans 1. He talks about how even unbelievers—rank pagans, we might say—have the yearning to worship. Without being told, without being commanded, without pondering God's revelation in Holy Scripture, they know they need to worship.

---

2. John Calvin, *Institutes of the Christian Religion*, trans. Ford Lewis Battles (Philadelphia: Westminster Press, 1960), 1.3.1.

But rather than worship something that is transcendentally true, good, and beautiful, they worship their sinful selves and things they have sinfully made:

> For the wrath of God is revealed from heaven against all ungodliness and unrighteousness of men, who suppress the truth in unrighteousness, because what may be known of God is manifest in them, for God has shown it to them. For since the creation of the world His invisible attributes are clearly seen, being understood by the things that are made, even His eternal power and Godhead, so that they are without excuse, because, although they knew God, they did not glorify Him as God, nor were thankful, but became futile in their thoughts, and their foolish hearts were darkened. Professing to be wise, they became fools, and changed the glory of the incorruptible God into an image made like corruptible man—and birds and four-footed animals and creeping things.
>
> Therefore God also gave them up to uncleanness, in the lusts of their hearts, to dishonor their bodies among themselves, who exchanged the truth of God for the lie, and worshiped and served the creature rather than the Creator, who is blessed forever. Amen. (Rom. 1:18–25)

Consider the point Paul is making in the opening and closing verses of this passage: the truth of God is suppressed, but worship is not. We will worship whether we like it or not because this is how we were made. The least religious people in the world are still worshipers.

A Worthwhile Endeavor
Philosopher James K. A. Smith at Calvin University approaches the subject of worship in a way that is refreshing and insightful.[3] Smith argues that we order our lives around what we want, and whatever we want we worship. As humans, we are not primarily thinking things (what Smith calls "brains on a stick"), but rather we are wanting-and-worshiping things. Augustine writes in his *Confessions*: "Wherever I am carried, my

---

3. James K. A. Smith, *You Are What You Love: The Spiritual Power of Habit* (Grand Rapids: Brazos Press, 2019), 1–25.

love is carrying me."[4] We desire things that we think will give us a good life—*the* good life, even—and so we order our lives around whatever that thing may be. That desiring and ordering is called worshiping.

Whatever is most important in our lives will be the thing we worship—which is just an inverse way of saying that worship is the most important thing we do in our lives. Reformer Martin Luther once wrote, "Whatever your heart clings to and confides in, that is really your god."[5] As the apostle Paul makes clear in Romans 1, the problem with the world is that so many people have made creaturely things their gods. These things are worthless—a fitting contrast to God when we consider that the word *worship* comes from the Old English *worth-ship*; that is, something which is inherently worthy. He alone is worthy to receive all glory and honor and power (Rev. 4:11).

Wanted: Worshipers
Moreover, we find evidence of the importance of worship in the sheer fact that ever since the fall, God has been in the business of reclaiming one thing: worshipers. The plan of redemption is a plan to get human-kind back to their created purpose of glorifying and enjoying God. Jesus says to the Samaritan woman at the well, "But the hour is coming, and now is, when the true worshipers will worship the Father in spirit and truth; for the Father is seeking such to worship Him. God is Spirit, and those who worship Him must worship in spirit and truth" (John 4:23–24). In his work *O Come, Let Us Worship*, Robert G. Rayburn says that this line from Jesus is "without parallel in all His teaching":

> Nowhere in all the Scriptures do we read of God's *seeking* anything else from the child of God.... Nowhere in the Bible are we told that the Lord seeks our service.... Nowhere do the Scriptures tell us that the Lord is seeking witnesses.... It is not without real significance that the only time in the Scriptures when the word *seek* is used of God's activity is in connection with seeking true worshippers.[6]

---

4. As quoted in Smith, *You Are What You Love*, 15.
5. As quoted in Smith, *You Are What You Love*, 23.
6. Robert G. Rayburn, *O Come, Let Us Worship* (Grand Rapids: Baker, 1980), 15–16, emphasis original.

God is seeking to reclaim a humanity that does what it was designed to do. He seeks to rekindle that inward sense of deity. He comes to point that inward tug, pull, yearning, desire that we all have in the right direction: toward Him. He comes to judge truth suppressors, but He also comes to seek, reclaim, and remake truth lovers. So we see that worship is the most important thing that we will ever do because it's the thing we were made for—and the thing we are being remade for.

Eternal Destiny
Beyond our being wired to worship, we find further proof of the all-importance of this duty when we consider that worship is the primary activity that extends from this world to the next. We could call this the argument from our *eternal destiny.* While the new heavens and the new earth will hold for the elect much more than an eternally sustained worship service—for we will eat, rest, fellowship, and much more—worship is undoubtedly the supreme undertaking of the believer in glory.

Where We Are Going and What We Will Be Doing There
We are given a glimpse into this reality several times in the book of Revelation (see 4:10–11; 5:11–14). On two occasions John is so moved by what he sees in his vision that he wants to bow to the angel who is before him, each time being reprimanded that he is to worship God alone (19:10; 22:9). In chapter 14, we are told that an angel proclaims an eternal gospel all over the earth, and this proclamation is not what we might expect (an explicit message of salvation in Jesus Christ). Rather, the angel says in a "loud voice": "Fear God and give glory to Him…and worship Him" (v. 7).

The scenes in Revelation also help us to see how it is *corporate* worship in particular that is to be preeminent in our lives rather than worship in a general sense. Certainly, our entire lives are to be lived as an act of worship (Rom. 12:1–2), but there is something unique about corporate worship. Corporate worship—that is, coming together with a body of believers regularly on Sunday to offer praise to God—is a picture of what goes on in heaven. This cannot be said of private worship. In heaven, we worship as a redeemed body, numbering thousands upon thousands. So we cannot excuse ourselves from worship in the church and think we are still fulfilling God's desire for His people. The church's number one task is to worship God, and we need to be a part of that.

The Mission of the Church

Did you know the church's primary task is worship? Some people may balk at this proposition. After all, isn't the church's task laid out very clearly by Jesus Himself in Matthew 28:19–20? "Go therefore and make disciples of all the nations, baptizing them in the name of the Father and of the Son and of the Holy Spirit, teaching them to observe all things that I have commanded you; and lo, I am with you always, even to the end of the age." A cursory glance at the Great Commission could make one think that evangelism, not worship, is the number one task of the church. But is the primary thrust of the Great Commission the verb "to go"?

Actually, the main verb in Matthew 28:19 is the imperative to "make disciples."[7] Indeed, there is the imperative "to go" as well, but to understand the Great Commission as merely "going" or "evangelizing" is to have a too narrow view of what Jesus was instructing. In their book *With Reverence and Awe*, Darryl Hart and John Muether write that "the Great Commission is not only about evangelism, nor is it mainly about evangelism. It is bigger."[8] We do not want to pit the various commands in the Great Commission against each other, but it is helpful to prioritize them. We must *go*—without leaving we will have no hope of finding, let alone making, disciples. Disciples cannot be made apart from evangelism. But that is only the beginning of the process. Discipleship grows deepest in the context of worship. We are trained up in the faith and mature in our understanding of the things of God by engaging in biblically robust worship week in and week out. After all, where do baptism and teaching (the word *didasko* is often used as a synonym for preaching in public gatherings) properly take place? In the church. Therefore "it is the *church*, and specifically the

---

7. Kevin DeYoung and Greg Gilbert, *What Is the Mission of the Church? Making Sense of Social Justice, Shalom, and the Great Commission* (Wheaton, Ill.: Crossway, 2011), 46.

8. Darryl G. Hart and John R. Muether, *With Reverence and Awe: Returning to the Basics of Reformed Worship* (Phillipsburg, N.J.: P&R, 2002), 47.

church at worship, that fulfills the Great Commission."⁹ Far from favoring evangelism at the expense of the worship of the church, the Great Commission shows that evangelism properly serves the worship of the church. Craig Troxel helpfully writes, "If the church begins to define herself in terms of her tasks and mission, this will significantly distort her self-understanding and potentially displace her primary function, the worship of God."¹⁰

The church has three tasks, or purposes: worship, discipleship, and missions. That the church is called to these three works is beyond dispute. The trouble is seeing how worship can be the primary purpose, especially when discipleship and missions are so blatantly spelled out in the Great Commission. We have explored how worship really lies behind all that the Great Commission is about. But this primacy of worship becomes even clearer when we consider our eternal destiny— that is, when we consider what we will be doing for ages without end in heaven. Discipleship, education, spiritual maturation will all pass away, for there and then we will know as we are known (1 Cor. 13:12). Evangelism and missions will pass away, for all the elect will be gathered and every knee will bow before King Jesus (Phil. 2:9–11). But worship, praise, and exaltation will remain. "Worship abides forever," says John Piper in his book on missions, *Let the Nations Be Glad!* He writes, "Missions is not the ultimate goal of the church. Worship is. Missions exists because God is ultimate, not man. When this age is over, and the countless millions of the redeemed fall on their faces before the throne of God, missions will be no more. It is a temporary necessity. But worship abides forever. Missions exists because worship doesn't."¹¹

We must also see that exaltation is the fount from which discipleship and evangelism flow. The primary means of witness and kingdom expansion comes from the free offer of the gospel proclaimed in the

9. Hart and Muether, *With Reverence and Awe*, 48, emphasis original.

10. A. Craig Troxel, "The World Is Not Enough: The Priority of the Church in Christ's Cosmic Headship," in *Confident of Better Things: Essays Commemorating Seventy-Five Years of the Orthodox Presbyterian Church*, ed. John R. Muether and Danny E. Olinger (Willow Grove, Pa.: Committee for the Historian of the Orthodox Presbyterian Church, 2011), 360.

11. John Piper, *Let the Nations Be Glad!: The Supremacy of God in Missions* (Grand Rapids: Baker Academic, 2010), 17.

preaching of the word. The primary means of edification and discipleship comes through the exhortation and explanation of Scripture in the context of the rhythms of corporate worship. In other words, if we do not worship properly, we will not witness properly. If we do not worship properly, we will not be walking in step with the Spirit and growing in Christian maturity.

One Thing Remains

I hope this makes it abundantly clear why it is true that worship is the most important thing you will ever do with your time here on earth. Nothing else has eternal significance like worship. We might even consider what we do every Sunday as "practice" for that great day in glory. Not only that, but this means that every week God is giving us a taste of the bliss and blessedness that await us in glory. This is so like our God: always lavishing us with that which we do not deserve and sustaining our present troubles with future delights. By so doing God graciously reminds us of where we are going and to keep our heads up. "God's gift to His sorrowing creatures," the consummate musician J. S. Bach once observed, "is to give them Joy worthy of their destiny."[12] The wonder of worship is but a small taste of the wonder of the new heavens and the new earth, and it is sufficient to sustain our hearts until we are there.

Therefore, our hearts should be tuned toward heaven every Lord's Day, and we should have an earnest desire to join the redeemed host:

> O that with yonder sacred throng
> we at His feet may fall;
> we'll join the everlasting song,
> and crown Him Lord of all.[13]

---

12. As quoted in Marva J. Dawn, *Reaching Out without Dumbing Down: A Theology of Worship for the Turn-of-the-Century Culture* (Grand Rapids: Eerdmans, 1995), 57.

13. Edward Perronet, "All Hail the Power of Jesus' Name" (1780), in *Trinity Hymnal*, rev. ed. (Suwanee, Ga.: Great Commission Publications, 1990).

Discussion Questions

1. Defend the statement that worship is the most important thing we could ever do.

2. What is the "sense of deity"? What is a Scripture passage that speaks about it?

3. What does John 4:23–24 teach us about the importance of worship?

4. What is the threefold mission of the church? Which of these is most important and why?

5. What does the activity of the church in heaven teach us about the activity of the church on earth?

Chapter 3

We Are Being Shaped

It is not by change of place that we can come nearer to Him who is in every place, but by the cultivation of pure desires and virtuous habits.
—Augustine

Do you have a morning routine? I don't really have one worth mentioning—getting out of bed and out the door on time is a victory for me any morning. But maybe you're like my much more disciplined friend who wakes up every morning at five, reads his Bible, tidies the house, goes for a three-mile run, comes back home and makes breakfast for the family—all before heading out the door for work around eight. This process has become so ingrained that to skip any step would cause him to feel "off" the rest of the day.

In this example, what has happened? My friend has trained himself to believe that this is what a good start to the day entails. By doing the same thing over and over again, he has trained himself to believe this is inherently good and right. This is true for us in all the habits that we form. Generally, we do not believe something first and then form a habit. Rather, we form a habit and then believe something. The more we do something, the harder it becomes to live without it. We have everyday habits that tell us the good life entails following certain practices. I want to read a good book in my chair at night because that's what I've always done and therefore that means it's good. I have been formed to believe this is what it means to end an evening well. Habits *shape* us.

The same is certainly true for the act of worship. If we are asking what happens when we worship, the answer we want to consider now is that we are being shaped. Something is literally happening *to* us when we fall into the practice of worship—this is true by the mere act of worship, no matter what the object of that worship may be. If the object of our worship is worthy (namely, the living God), then we are training ourselves for something good: to prepare for our ultimate end of eternally worshiping our Maker. Conversely, a poor object of worship results in poor practice. We end up training ourselves for something quite bad: preparing to meet that very same Maker, only this time for eternal judgment. This understanding of the formative power of worship caused Marva Dawn to write with such urgency that her "major concern for the Church has to do with worship, because its character-forming potential is so subtle and barely noticed, and yet worship creates a great impact on the hearts and minds and lives of a congregation's members. Indeed, how we worship both reveals and forms our identity as persons and communities."[1]

So we need to recognize how often we have been shaped by the wrong kind of worship, have formed the wrong kinds of loves and desires, and set a course to correct it. And true, sincere, reverent Christian corporate worship is the place to do just that.

We Become Like What We Worship

It is a scary thought when you consider that there is so much in the world that clamors for our attention and bids us to come and worship. There is the entertainment culture, which says we need to be occupied and amused every second of every day—*this* is the good life. The fashion world says how you dress and how you look is ultimate—*this* is the good life. The business end of things tells you that work and money and success and power and influence are all that matter—*this* is the good life. And then we start to worship these things. We order our lives around these things. And there's a vicious cycle here: the more we order our lives around things we want, the more we form habits, and when habits take control, we crave even more. The habits that we set for ourselves train us to love with even deeper ardor and desire.

---

1. Dawn, *Reaching Out without Dumbing Down*, 4.

We will be changed and transformed and shaped into whatever it is that we find to be of the utmost importance in this life. What are our ultimate desires? Fame? Sex and pleasure? Family? Health? If we worship it, we will become like it. This is not just some clever insight; this is what the Bible teaches:

> The idols of the nations are silver and gold,
> The work of men's hands.
> They have mouths, but they do not speak;
> Eyes they have, but they do not see;
> They have ears, but they do not hear;
> Nor is there any breath in their mouths.
> *Those who make them are like them*;
> So is everyone who trusts in them. (Ps. 135:15–18;
>   cf. Ps. 115:4–8, which uses nearly the same language)

This is an extremely important text to learn when considering the topic of worship. What does it teach us? Here the Lord condemns all the idolatrous worship of the pagan nations by basically making one argument: it's foolish. It makes no sense. Why worship something you yourself have made, which would mean you are submitting to something you have ultimate authority over? Why worship and bow down to something made of wood or stone that can't speak, can't hear—essentially, why bow down and worship anything other than the one true and living God? What has happened here is what Paul writes about in Romans 1, which we considered in the last chapter: "[They] worshiped and served the creature rather than the Creator, who is blessed forever" (v. 25).

God's condemnation against these idols is that they are dumb, stupid, lifeless creatures. There is no worth in them; therefore they lack the requisite of worship (worth-ship). But what does God say next? He says that those who worship such creatures will become like them: dumb, stupid, lifeless as well. We become what we behold—and in the case of those who behold idols, this is not a good thing. We see as much in Isaiah 42:18–20:

> Hear, you deaf;
> And look, you blind, that you may see.
> Who is blind but My servant,

Or deaf as My messenger whom I send?
Who is blind as he who is perfect,
And blind as the LORD's servant?
Seeing many things, but you do not observe;
Opening the ears, but he does not hear.

The insult against a rebellious nation is to say that they have become just like the idols they have formed and worshiped.

But this is exactly what worship does. It shapes us. It takes what we love and trains us in how to love it more. Worship both reflects what matters to us and shapes what matters to us.[2] Worship trains and transforms. Worship does something to us. Is it doing something good to us? Something that will prepare us for the true good life of glory? Or is it training us for a weak imitation of the good life that will only leave us unsatisfied?

Cattle Cult

Consider two instances from Scripture where we are given contrasting examples of how this can play out in either positive or negative ways. The first example comes from Exodus 32–34 and the incident of the golden calf. Moses is on top of Mount Sinai receiving the covenant law from God. Meanwhile, at the base of the mountain the people have grown impatient. They prove that our innate desire is for worship, for they cannot even hold back this desire long enough for Moses to return and give them instructions on how to properly worship their God. Instead, they fashion idols in the form of two golden calves. Granted, the people do not grow tails, horns, and hooves and start mooing. But when Moses comes down from the mountaintop and sees their wickedness, how does he rebuke the people? In terms fitting for ignorant, untrained, and stubborn cattle! They are called a "stiff-necked people" who have "turned aside quickly out of the way," like cattle that won't obey the bridle (32:8–9; 33:3, 5; 34:9), and they have broken loose and need to be regathered (32:25–26).

---

2. James K. A. Smith, *Desiring the Kingdom: Worship, Worldview, and Cultural Formation* (Grand Rapids: Baker Academic, 2009), 93.

Conversely, as Moses climbs back up to the mountain to speak with God, he too is transformed—not into a dumb bovine, though. As he worships the One who is true and honorable and glorious, he is transformed to reflect the very same: "When Moses came down from Mount Sinai, with the two tablets of the testimony in his hand as he came down from the mountain, Moses did not know that the skin of his face shone because he had been talking with God" (34:29 ESV). The Israelites are depicted as becoming like their idols; Moses like his God.

Producing a Prophet

Another example is from Isaiah 6, the famous scene in which the prophet beholds the glory and holiness of God and is undone because of his sin. But by beholding his God, Isaiah deals with his sin. He actually takes on the quality of the One whom he is worshiping: holiness. He says,

> "Woe is me, for I am undone!
> Because I am a man of unclean lips,
> And I dwell in the midst of a people of unclean lips;
> For my eyes have seen the King,
> The LORD of hosts."

> Then one of the seraphim flew to me, having in his hand a live coal which he had taken with the tongs from the altar. And he touched my mouth with it, and said:
>> "Behold, this has touched your lips;
>> Your iniquity is taken away,
>> And your sin purged." (Isa. 6:5–7)

But while Isaiah is sanctified, it is for the purpose of then calling down God's judgment on the rest of the people who have given in to idolatrous practices. His commission is to rebuke a people for having ears but not hearing, eyes but not seeing. It's nearly the exact language of Psalm 115. So in Isaiah 6 we see a people called out for being deformed by their idolatrous worship and a lone prophet summoned by God and graciously conformed to mirror His holiness.

We become like what we worship—for good or bad. G. K. Beale has put it memorably: "What people revere they resemble, either for their ruin or their restoration."[3] This is, in short, the power of liturgy.

The Power of Liturgy

What do you think of when you hear the term *liturgy*? Oftentimes we conjure up images of the Roman Catholic Mass or some other type of interminable, formal worship service that involves robes and kneelers and the whole nine yards. But that's more of a caricature than it is an accurate depiction of what liturgy is. We get *liturgy* from the Greek *leitourgia*, which is a combination of two Greek words: people (*laos*) and work (*ergon*). Literally, a liturgy is a "work of the people," or a "public service." Therefore, at its most basic, *liturgy* refers to the order of a corporate worship service.

Every Church Is Liturgical

There is no such thing as a nonliturgical church. Everyone has a liturgy. If your church worships, you follow a liturgy. There is no church where the people do not come together to perform some kind of work or service. A church may open their service with announcements, sing for a half hour, have some time of prayer, then maybe a quick sermonette, and conclude with more singing and claim they are not liturgical. But what I have just laid out—a service you can find in nearly any mainstream evangelical church today—is a liturgy.

When churches say they are not liturgical, what they usually mean is that they do not follow a historic pattern of worship, which is not the same thing. Or it may mean that they do not take their order of worship very seriously. It's not that important to them. They may have an "anything goes" mentality. But whatever "goes"—even if it varies from week to week—is still a liturgy. On the other hand, if a church claims to be liturgical, or perhaps even highly liturgical, this simply means they have thought about their order of worship and care about the elements

---

3. G. K. Beale, *We Become What We Worship* (Downers Grove, Ill.: InterVarsity, 2008), 16. The examples of Moses and Isaiah are treated in depth in this work as well on pages 76–86 and 36–70, respectively.

therein much more. But in the proper sense of the term, no church is more liturgical than any other.

What's important to recognize, though, is that the way a liturgy is shaped will determine how we are shaped. As we've seen, worship is a very formative thing. Therefore, "the goal of a liturgy is for the participant to be formed in a certain way," says Justin Whitmel Earley in his book on habits.[4] We must then ask the question, Is the worship that we participate in on a regular basis—the worship that we habituate—forming us in the right ways, for the right reasons, into the right people?

Cultural Liturgies

Liturgy is a powerful thing in that way. James Smith has a provocative spin on this: he says that our world is full of secular or cultural liturgies—orders of worship that are training us to yearn for a certain form of the good life. These are subtle. Remember, we are not primarily thinking creatures; we base decisions on our gut. Smith says everywhere we turn we are confronted with liturgies that are shaping us at an unconscious level: the mall, the university, the stadium, and so forth.

Take the mall, for example. It preaches to us the reality of our sin in thinking we don't have enough; we don't have the newest and best thing. This makes us broken. But we are presented with a "gospel" as well: we can have the newest and best thing if we come to the mall and shop. There is the "hope of redemption through consumption." Like other worshiping communities, the mall has a social aspect, but it can also be as private as we'd prefer it to be (no doubt with the rise of Amazon Prime even consumeristic worship is transforming from a public activity to a private one). We present our offerings (merchandise) at the altar (the counter) and the priest (the cashier) gratefully accepts them and sends us off with a benediction and a reminder to come and worship again soon. But the good life that is presented here is never attainable. What we buy will go out of style, and we will need more and more and more. Nevertheless, we can be easily trained in the worship of consumerism.[5]

---

4. Justin Whitmel Earley, *The Common Rule: Habits of Purpose for an Age of Distraction* (Downers Grove, Ill.: InterVarsity, 2019), 8.

5. For Smith's extended "cultural exegesis," see *Desiring the Kingdom*, 93–103.

A Liturgy for the (Real) Good Life

This is just one example of how we are involved in inherently worshipful practices in our everyday lives, almost entirely on the subconscious
level. Without thinking about it, we give in to what the world tells us
is ultimate, is happiness, is necessary. As Christians, though, we have
another idea of the good life. It's not just an idea of it, not just an ideal—
it's a reality. We know that a life of obedience to our great God will
mean blessings in abundance (Ps. 1:3). And yet what we see is that there
is this conflict in our lives, in every week, in almost everything we do.
It's a conflict between worship (what the world trains us for) and Worship (what the church is to train us for).

We've seen the power of liturgy. We've seen the power of habit.
We've seen that our loves are cultivated through patterns and repeti-
tions. We can't simply tell ourselves to do what's right because we are
not primarily thinking things. We need to be shown. We need to experience. We need to see, taste, and touch. Thomas Cranmer, author of
the Book of Common Prayer, is often credited with this line: "What the
heart loves, the will chooses, and then the mind justifies." This is a profoundly insightful remark, and terrifying if you think about it. Notice
what he says: we do what we love, and our brains will catch up later.
This is all well and good if our hearts love the right thing. But what if we
are in love with sinful lusts and passions or ideals of the good life that
are ultimately not satisfying? We need to be retrained. And this is part
of what Sunday worship is all about.

Think about it: all week, Monday through Saturday, the world tells
you what matters most and what you should want. And no matter how
hard you may try, you can't escape it. You might not watch TV or use
Facebook, but things still seep in. We start doing things as a culture
because it's just what we do. But Sunday is the time when we are being
retrained. Sunday worship is (or should be) the time when we are told
about and trained for the real good life. This takes careful thought. If
we decide to have our worship services look however we think they
should look, you know what will happen? They'll resemble the world,
and it will become idolatry. We will be the deaf, dumb, and blind people
in Isaiah 42. Rather, we need to see what the Scripture says about the
shape of our worship in order for us to be shaped into the people that

we are meant to be. Again, James Smith is right on: "Christian worship needs to be intentionally liturgical, formative, and pedagogical in order to *counter* such misinformation and misdirections. While the practices of Christian worship are best understood as the restoration of an original, creational desire for God, practically speaking, Christian worship functions as a counter-formation to the mis-formation of secular liturgies into which we are 'thrown' from an early age.... Christian liturgy functions as a counter-formation."[6]

We can't just think our way out of bad habits. If that were true, then you and I would leave Sunday after the sermon as entirely changed people, right? After all, we just heard how much God has done for us and how He wants us to live. We know what we need to know—that should be enough. But it isn't! So often the change that we want to implement Sunday afternoon has already failed by Sunday evening. Why? Because we are not primarily thinking things. We are creatures that go with their gut, their desires. Michael Horton says this:

> Even if we are lifelong Christians, we forget why we came to church this Sunday until it all happens again: we come in with our shallow scripts that are formed out of the clippings in our imaginations from the ads and celebrities of the last week, only to be reintroduced to our real script and to find ourselves by losing ourselves all over again. It is not merely as we entertain the possibility of being a character in this story, or some other purely subjective strategy, that this narrative has the dramatic power to reconstitute us. Rather, it is as God the Spirit works on us through the proclamation of the Word that we are rescripted: our lives, purposes, identities, and hopes conformed to that "new world" into which the Word and Spirit give us new birth—instead of the other way around. Instead of our remaking God and His Word in terms of our experience and reason, we end up being remade— caught up in the action of the divine drama.[7]

---

6. Smith, *Desiring the Kingdom*, 88.
7. Michael Scott Horton, *A Better Way: Rediscovering the Drama of God-Centered Worship* (Grand Rapids: Baker Books, 2002), 52.

That's what happens to us in worship: we come to be reformed, reshaped, remade. Hughes Oliphant Old says that "worship is the workshop where we are transformed into [God's] image. When we are thus transformed into his image, we then reflect his glory."[8] We come to worship in order to "put on the Lord Jesus Christ" (Rom. 13:14).

We have a hard time remembering that this refining work is what goes on during the Sunday service. We can oftentimes think we are sitting around wasting an hour or two of our weekend—and for what? We likely wouldn't make that complaint if we made regular trips to the gym. Regular, habitual exercise produces visible results: loss of weight, toned muscles, increased endurance. But even if we can't quite see them, the same things are happening in worship! We lose the weight of sin, we are toned and sharpened in our understanding of the living word of God, and we are granted endurance to run our race of faith. In short, corporate worship is where we are conformed to mature manhood, "to a perfect man, to the measure of the stature of the fullness of Christ" (Eph. 4:13).

From Dust to Glory

So this has to be what we are pursuing in our worship services: a liturgy that is rooted in God's story of redemption, simultaneously forming within us a desire for the true good life and conforming us to attain it. It must be a liturgy that is rooted in the gospel. The gospel is not merely a message to be heard but it's a life to be lived. Worship should be a time when we are led in that lifestyle. Seeking to know Jesus more intimately means engaging in practices that will help us see all the ways in which He is true, good, and beautiful. Those are the kinds of habits that true worship should form within us. This will set the proper course for the rest of our week. As Michael Horton writes, "Whatever fills our Sundays fills our hearts throughout the week."[9] He goes on, "Filled with the intensity of such sovereign grace the Lord's Day becomes a beachhead

---

8. Hughes Oliphant Old, *Worship: Reformed according to Scripture* (Louisville: Westminster John Knox, 2002), 8.

9. Michael Horton, *Ordinary: Sustainable Faith in a Radical, Restless World* (Grand Rapids: Zondervan, 2014), 177.

for the transformation of our whole lives, so that every day is warmed by its light."[10]

Recall the biblical principle that was laid out for us in Psalms 115 and 135: we will become like what we worship. And God's will for us is that we become like Him:

> Therefore, since we have such hope, we use great boldness of speech—unlike Moses, who put a veil over his face so that the children of Israel could not look steadily at the end of what was passing away. But their minds were blinded. For until this day the same veil remains unlifted in the reading of the Old Testament, because the veil is taken away in Christ. But even to this day, when Moses is read, a veil lies on their heart. Nevertheless when one turns to the Lord, the veil is taken away. Now the Lord is the Spirit; and where the Spirit of the Lord is, there is liberty. But we all, with unveiled face, beholding as in a mirror the glory of the Lord, are being transformed into the same image from glory to glory, just as by the Spirit of the Lord. (2 Cor. 3:12–18)

The apostle Paul is writing here about new covenant worship. That is, he's writing about the worship that you and I partake in. And what does he say? The Spirit is present in our worship. And this is how we may behold the Lord Himself: through His Spirit in His Word. And as we behold the Lord, guess what? We become like Him! "We all, with unveiled face, beholding as in a mirror the glory of the Lord, are being transformed into the same image." We are shaped and transformed to be more and more like Him. We answer the purpose for which we were made: to be the image of God.

So now several questions are laid before us: Do our services of worship shape us to be like the Creator or like creation? Are we being fashioned for earth or for heaven? Do we walk away from worship looking more like dust or more like glory? Charles Wesley gives us beautiful words that make a fitting prayer for worship:

> Finish, then, thy new creation;
> pure and spotless let us be:

---

10. Horton, *Ordinary*, 199.

let us see thy great salvation
perfectly restored in thee;
changed from glory into glory,
'til in heav'n we take our place,
'til we cast our crowns before thee,
lost in wonder, love, and praise.[11]

Discussion Questions

1. Explain what it means that we become what we worship, using examples from Scripture.

2. What does the word *liturgy* mean?

3. In what way is every church liturgical?

4. What kind of liturgy does your church have?

5. How can we ensure that we are being transformed and shaped in the right ways?

---

11. Charles Wesley, "Love Divine, All Loves Excelling" (1747), in *Trinity Hymnal.*

Chapter 4

We Meet with God

Public worship is the nearest resemblance of heaven.
—David Clarkson

As I stated at the close of the previous chapter, the reason that true Christian worship shapes us into something for our restoration (as opposed to our ruin) is because in true Christian worship we actually meet with God. Let that thought sink in for a moment: *we meet with God.*

When the saints gather on God's appointed day and worship Him in the way that He has directed (more on that in the next chapter), *God is actually there.* We literally come into His presence. It's hard to believe, isn't it? In something that seems as mundane as a church service, we are actually given the opportunity to come before the living God, the Creator of the universe, the holy, self-sufficient, transcendent God. We meet Him, really and truly. If it weren't for this, Christian worship would be quite meaningless. It would be, I daresay, a waste of your time—especially when the world is urging you to catch the big game that day instead. But because we meet with God, everything changes. Corporate worship becomes the greatest means of making us into what we were always meant to be: the image bearers of God. We are reflective creatures who become like what we behold—and in Christian worship we behold God.

But let's unpack what exactly it means that God is present in worship. No doubt there are some objections to or, at the very least, questions about this claim.

Can't We Meet with God Anytime and Anywhere We Want?
There are many people, Christians or not, who would love the chance
to meet with God. These people might be characteristically described
as "spiritual but not religious." Maybe you've met them before. Maybe
you would consider yourself this type of individual: one who is eager
for an existential experience where the divine and human can connect.
This popular desire fuels entire tourist industries. Sedona, Arizona,
is frequented heavily by people who travel from all over the world to
experience the so-called spiritual vortexes that cover the area. According to Sedona's tourist website, spiritual vortexes are "swirling centers of
energy that are conducive to healing, meditation and self-exploration."
People think that's the extent of religion. They think that's meeting with
God. They believe these natural phenomena are how you meet with a
supernatural being.

I've heard this kind of thing from countless people. They don't
go to church per se, but the outdoors is their church. "Just give me a
hammock under the starry night sky and some solitude—that's all the
church I need," they say. People seem to think church is hardly that
important when you can meet with God camping, or perhaps at an art
exhibit, or while taking your morning jog. "I am with God cozied up on
my couch with a good book and some delicious coffee just as much as
if I were at worship." It sounds nice, but it's not true.

Am I saying that God is not present in any of these other venues?
No, of course not. We believe one of God's essential attributes is His
omnipresence: He is everywhere present all the time always. There isn't
a single nook or cranny in this universe that escapes God's presence
(Ps. 139:7–10). All things are from and through Him, and in Him all
things hold together (Rom. 11:36; Col. 1:17). So, yes, God is present
everywhere. But here's the thing: God does not promise to meet with
people everywhere. He doesn't take appointments at any place we would
choose. You might run into your doctor at the grocery store, but that
doesn't mean she will give you an exam right there and then! For that,
you make an appointment at the office. So too, God's primary method
is to meet with His people at His house—at church! This is where He
has guaranteed us He can be found. It is in worship where we can know
for certain that we will meet with God.

T. David Gordon gives a wonderful and whimsical example of this. Once on a hike in New Hampshire he spotted a dime on the trail. It was nice to find an extra ten cents, but Gordon says that if you were a coin collector and were actually looking for dimes, you would hardly go searching on a hiking trail on Mount Lafayette. You might find a dime there, but if you go to a bank you know you'll find a dime—and plenty of them. So it is with finding God:

> So when you're present with those who praise and adore God, who acknowledge their sins, who thank him for his dying and rising Son, that's where you meet God now. Later [in the next life], we meet Him in other kinds of ways, but that's where we meet Him now. So what we call "worship" could also be called "meeting with God," and we could call our assemblies "God's house," because the apostles call it God's house. Peter does, Paul does, the author to Hebrews does. Those assemblies, and those who gather there, are called God's house, and that's where He is to be met, if we wish to meet Him in this life. Might we find Him, on occasion, somewhere else? Yes, you can sometimes find a dime on a mountaintop.[1]

An Important Clarification

Now, don't take this illustration too far. Gordon is specifically promoting the practice of corporate worship in the context of those who would reject the importance of the assembly. He is not denying that we encounter God through other means like private prayer or group Bible study. He is not downplaying the significance and need of such things as personal or family worship. Private and family worship are vital to one's spiritual life and real ways that we come to grow in our relationship with God. But the point I'm seeking to make in this chapter, and indeed the whole book, is that of the necessity and supremacy of corporate worship.[2] "Public worship is to be preferred before private. So it is by the Lord, so it should be by his people." This was the conclusion

---

1. T. David Gordon, "Biblical Theology and the 'House of Prayer' in Worship," in *On Reforming Worship*, ed. David W. Hall and Jonathan L. Master (Powder Springs, Ga.: Covenant Foundation, 2018), 61.

2. For further study of the importance of family worship in particular, I would recommend two helpful sources: Joel Beeke, *Family Worship* (Grand Rapids: Reformation

drawn by English Puritan David Clarkson in his famous treatise expos-
iting Psalm 87:2 (KJV), "The LORD loveth the gates of Zion more than
all the dwellings of Jacob."[3] Moreover, it is what goes on at church on
Sundays that feeds and fuels our private and family devotions throughout the week. Without corporate worship, these other means would die.

With Gordon I affirm that God can meet with us in some pretty
extraordinary ways. In Reformed theology we refer to what goes on in
worship as the "*ordinary* means of grace," not the "*only* means of grace."
Extraordinary encounters happen—just ask Paul about his Damascus
road experience. Yes, you can sometimes find a dime on a mountaintop.
But that random event should not establish a habit for your pursuits
as a coin collector. So too, true believers build their relationship with
God on the certainty of meeting with Him at His house, not on the vain
hopes of running into Him somewhere else.

Meeting with God in the Old Testament
Your ancient believing Israelite wouldn't bat an eye at the claim that
corporate worship is a meeting with God. They believed it wholeheartedly, for He told them as much. God was visibly present in marvelous
ways to the people of Israel as they made their exodus from Egypt and
journeyed through the wilderness. A pillar of cloud by day and a pillar of fire by night proved that God was with them. But if the Israelites
wanted to actually meet with God, really have a personal encounter with
Him, God allocated His presence to a particular place: the tabernacle.

The house of worship is where God could be reached. So we read in
Exodus 25:8, "Let them make Me a sanctuary, that I may dwell among
them." And even more specifically, within that sanctuary God was to be
found at the ark of the covenant: "You shall put the mercy seat on top of
the ark, and in the ark you shall put the Testimony that I will give you.

Heritage Books, 2009); and Jason Helopoulos, *A Neglected Grace: Family Worship in the Christian Home* (Fearn, Ross-shire, Scotland: Christian Focus, 2013).

3. David Clarkson, "Public Worship to Be Preferred Before Private," in *The Practical Works of David Clarkson* (Edinburgh: James Nichol, 1865), 3:187–209. The entire treatise is filled with wonderful, biblical arguments proving this important point, and anyone would benefit from engaging with it.

And there I will meet with you, and I will speak with you" (vv. 21–22). No wonder the tabernacle came to be called the tent of meeting!

Similarly, when the days of the tabernacle were over and Israel had settled in the promised land, God still would take appointments only at the place of worship. This was now the temple. The temple housed the ark of the covenant. And at the dedication of the temple, we read that as soon as Solomon concluded his dedication prayer, "fire came down from heaven and consumed the burnt offering and the sacrifices; and the glory of the LORD filled the temple. And the priests could not enter the house of the LORD, because the glory of the LORD had filled the LORD's house" (2 Chron. 7:1–2). This was even further proof that the temple was indeed God's house.

A Better Way
What about today? We don't have tabernacles, temples, or arks anymore. Does God still have a house? Does He still meet with us at church when we worship? The answer is yes! God's mode of meeting with His people is much simpler: no more pillars of cloud or consuming fire from heaven. No more washing or bloody sacrifices. And, as in most cases, simpler is better.

The author of Hebrews, drawing upon the practices of tabernacle worship, explains how we can now enter God's presence tabernacle-free through the work of Jesus Christ. The book answers two important aspects of new covenant worship: the *how* and the *where*. The *how* is Jesus.

How We Meet with God
In Hebrews 10:19–22, the author writes, "Therefore, brethren, having boldness to enter the Holiest by the blood of Jesus, by a new and living way which He consecrated for us, through the veil, that is, His flesh, and having a High Priest over the house of God, let us draw near with a true heart in full assurance of faith, having our hearts sprinkled from an evil conscience and our bodies washed with pure water." How can we enter the holy place of worship? According to this text, we have confidence to enter the holy place through the blood of Jesus. In the old covenant, if the people wanted to worship the living God, there had to be sacrifice.

There had to be blood—every single time. Not anymore: "Not with the blood of goats and calves, but with His own blood [Christ] entered the Most Holy Place once for all, having obtained eternal redemption" (9:12). The blood of bulls and goats has a poor shelf life. The perfect and precious blood of the Son of God, however, secures an eternal redemption and purifies for an eternal worship.

So we can enter the holy place because we have been cleansed through faith by the blood of our Great High Priest. In other words, it is our belief in the good news that makes us capable of worship. David Peterson writes that "drawing near to God means believing the gospel and…constantly expressing trust in Jesus and his saving work."[4] Jesus Christ is the key that opens to us the holy place of worship, and we enter the presence of God through faith in Him.

Where We Meet with God

But where exactly is the holy place? If the *how* of new covenant worship is Jesus, the *where* is heaven. In Hebrews 8:1–2 we read, "We have such a high priest, one who is seated at the right hand of the throne of the Majesty in heaven, a minister in the holy places, in the true tent that the Lord set up, not man" (ESV). Notice how the author of Hebrews equates the holy places with heaven. He also says that Christ is in "the true tent"—in other words, the real tent of meeting is in heaven. This is where real worship takes place. This is where we meet with God—no longer in temples made by man but in His heavenly sanctuary.

Did you know that when the people of God gather for corporate worship they are drawn by a mysterious work of the Holy Spirit into the heavenly places? That's what's happening when we worship, and that's where worship is happening. Hebrews 12 proves this point. There we read that when we come to worship, we actually don't come to what "may be touched," like the Israelites did when they worshiped at Mount Sinai (vv. 18–21). And if our worship location can't be touched, then that must mean it is a spiritual place. And indeed we are told that in worship we "have come to Mount Zion and to the city of the living

---

4. David Peterson, *Engaging with God: A Biblical Theology of Worship* (Downers Grove, Ill.: InterVarsity, 1992), 240–41.

God, *the heavenly Jerusalem*, to an innumerable company of angels, to the general assembly and church of the firstborn who are registered in heaven, to God the Judge of all, to the spirits of just men made perfect, to Jesus the Mediator of the new covenant, and to the blood of sprinkling that speaks better things than that of Abel" (vv. 22–24).

That's where we meet with God. It is in the heavenly Jerusalem, where there are angels and saints and, most importantly, God Himself! We don't see it. We can't touch it. It is spiritual. But it's real. By faith, that's where we are when we worship.

It should be noted that in God's wonderful wisdom this was always His intention for the location of worship. Even in the old covenant God was pointing His people forward to the reality that true worship and communion with Him would occur in the heavenly places. Moses and Aaron, Nadab and Abihu, and the elders of Israel climbing Mount Sinai to feast with God (Ex. 24:9) were types of the spiritual ascent our hearts make into heaven when we worship. The psalmist inquires, "Who may ascend into the hill of the LORD? Or who may stand in His holy place?" (Ps. 24:3). God was teaching His people that true worship must include an upward trajectory. What was foreshadowed in the old covenant then finds its fulfillment in the new.

In commenting on Jesus's encounter with the Samaritan woman in John 4, D. G. Hart writes, "In the new era of redemptive history, after the coming of Christ and the fulfillment of temple worship, God's people would no longer have to worry about worshiping in a special place or on a particular mountain." He goes on: "The worship in which Christians now participate is heavenly worship because it is spiritual worship, that is, it is worship filled with and dependent on the work of the Holy Spirit, not on the place of the worshiper."[5] I have heard a pastor say that if you could blow the roof off the sanctuary on a given Sunday and were given a glimpse into the heavenly worship that we are participating in, no one would ever doze off in church!

Do you want to meet with God? Then go to worship. Don't go on a hike. Don't go searching for some thrilling, moving experience.

---

5. D. G. Hart, *Recovering Mother Kirk: The Case for Liturgy in the Reformed Tradition* (Grand Rapids: Baker Academic, 2003), 93, 98.

Actually, God has promised to appear with us in some pretty ordinary ways: the preaching of the word, the administration of the sacraments, and prayer. The Westminster Confession of Faith 25.3 says that God has given these things to the church, and when they are rightly administered we are blessed "by [Jesus's] own presence" among us.

The Sacred and the Secular

I would seriously probe the motivation behind those who seek to remove themselves from the corporate body and practices of the church in favor of a more private communion with God. In these private disciplines, what is their desire? Is it to hear God speak to them? Or rather is it to cultivate a space where they can better hear themselves speak? Poet Ralph Waldo Emerson, champion of transcendentalism and individualism, wrote in his essay "Self-Reliance," "I like the silent church before the service begins, better than any preaching." Those who share Emerson's thinking on this see a time of calm and quiet reflection and introspection as a more divine and spiritual encounter than when God speaks to His gathered, corporate people through the preaching of His word.

Even though certain spiritual disciplines have their place in the Christian life, they are still not the most special, most sacred place to meet with God. Yes, we can pray wherever and whenever and know that God hears us. What a blessing! We can read our Bible on the train to work and know the Spirit is illuminating our hearts and minds. How astounding! But none of these things can substitute for corporate worship.

In her well-written book *Liturgy of the Ordinary*, Tish Harrison Warren does a fascinating job of comparing the motions of worship to the motions of our everyday lives. She excels at showing that worship is not necessarily the most exciting, flashiest thing, but that God uses it anyway. A weakness in her book, however, is in blurring the lines between the sacred and the secular, drawing the conclusion that the work God does in a corporate worship setting is the same work He does throughout the week. "God is forming us into a new people," she accurately writes. "And the place of that formation is in the small moments of today."[6] Throughout the book she shows those small moments when God meets with us and exercises His transformative power on us: while we make the bed, while we're stuck in traffic, while we fight with our spouse. It is undoubtedly true that God uses these everyday moments for our good and His glory (as He uses everything), but it is confusing to say they are "the place" where this work takes place. *The* place where God forms us into a new people, the primary location of that sanctifying work, is not in the small moments of every day; rather, it is in the seemingly mundane but truly wonderful moment of corporate worship.

We need to reclaim an appreciation for the unique place and purpose of the church in today's Christian culture. The church is Christ's bride, and it is in corporate worship that we are knit together and brought into communion with God and with one another. Reading the Bible is a vital practice for Christians, but recall the scene of Philip and the Ethiopian eunuch:

> So Philip ran to him, and heard him reading the prophet Isaiah, and said, "Do you understand what you are reading?"
>
> And he said, "How can I, unless someone guides me?"
> (Acts 8:30–31)

God gives us that guidance on Sundays, for He has chosen to use especially the preached word to reach the lost and disciple His children, and it is in corporate worship that the word is preached. Likewise, the sacraments were given to the church and are administered there, and there only. It's in corporate worship where we are lifted up into that heavenly worship service.[7]

This understanding has properly influenced the liturgy in some Christian services in Africa. At one point in the worship, the pastor asks the people, "Is God here?" They reply, "Yes, He is here!" I think that's a beautiful practice. With great joy we can affirm in worship that God is indeed with us because by His Spirit He has drawn us to Himself!

---

6. Tish Harrison Warren, *Liturgy of the Ordinary* (Downers Grove, Ill.: InterVarsity, 2016), 22.

7. I am largely indebted to my friend and father in the faith Bob Jackson for the formulation of this paragraph.

And that worship encounter can happen in any location, can't it? I have worshiped in ancient, breathtaking cathedrals and in modern sanctuaries with light systems and big screens. I have worshiped outdoors at a campground nestled in the mountains. I have participated in Christian worship services that were held in a Jewish synagogue, a Seventh-day Adventist sanctuary, and a high school gymnatorium. And in each instance I know that I have actually, in a mysterious yet marvelous spiritual reality, been in the heavenly places. And I know that I have met with God.

Discussion Questions

1. What would a thoughtful, caring, and nuanced reply be to someone who claims they don't need to go to church to meet with God?

2. How did the people of God meet with Him in the old covenant?

3. How do we meet with God in the new covenant?

4. In what ways may we have to distinguish between the secular and the sacred when it comes to encountering God and worshiping Him?

5. In what way can it be said we are in heaven when we worship?

Chapter 5

God Renews His Covenant

Men will never worship God with a sincere heart, or be roused to fear and obey him with sufficient zeal, until they properly understand how much they are indebted to his mercy.
—John Calvin

Meeting with God can sound like a pretty terrifying thing. And indeed, apart from Christ, it would be terrifying because we would have nothing to bring before the Creator of the universe but our sin and guilt. There is nothing we can bring Him that would appease His wrath for our disobedience. We would shrink in fear before Him. But in Christian worship, the opposite is true. We who are true believers can now "draw near with a true heart in full assurance of faith" (Heb. 10:22). And why? Because in Christian worship, God doesn't meet us with our guilt; He meets us with His grace.

We are going to discover in this chapter that the worship service is a sacred moment when God condescends to His sinful people and restores them to Himself. Even though we do not deserve His favor—and have done plenty to earn His wrath—God reminds us in worship that our relationship with Him is about His commitment to us, not our performance before Him. Put another way, through the steps of corporate worship God graciously renews His covenant faithfulness to us.

Covenant Relationship
The fact that we meet with God as believers means that we have a relationship with Him, and in the Bible the term for God's relationship with His creatures is *covenant*. More specifically, a covenant is a relationship

based on binding promises between at least two parties, usually one greater and one lesser. The greater party stoops down and establishes a bond with the lesser or weaker party. So a mighty king, known as a suzerain, might enter into a covenant with a weak tribe, called the vassal, promising them protection from their enemies if they swear allegiance to him and pay him taxes. In terms of our relationship with God, He enters into a covenant with us, promising us salvation when by grace we call on Him in faith. Worship takes place in this covenantal context. Meeting with God in worship is to engage in a covenantal conversation with the Great King. So we learn a lot about what is going on in worship when we examine God's covenantal dealings in Scripture.

This is true from the very beginning. In the garden of Eden, the first worship center, God expected perfect obedience from Adam and Eve. By creating them out of nothing and then giving them a command, God had condescended to them and constituted a covenantal relationship. They would have everlasting life if they obeyed: "Then the LORD God took the man and put him in the garden of Eden to tend and keep it. And the LORD God commanded the man, saying, 'Of every tree of the garden you may freely eat; but of the tree of the knowledge of good and evil you shall not eat, for in the day that you eat of it you shall surely die'" (Gen. 2:15–17). The sign of this everlasting life would be a feast: if Adam and Eve obeyed and did not eat of the forbidden fruit, they would be privileged to eat of the Tree of Life (3:22). Jonathan Gibson helpfully points out that we have here the seedling structure of all true covenantal worship: "for Adam and all his descendants a liturgy was fixed, stitched into the very order and fabric of human life on earth: call—response—meal. Call to worship (through God's Word), Response (by faith and obedience, love and devotion), Fellowship meal (union and communion with God). In short, worship in Eden was familial, covenantal communion."[1]

As I have already discussed in earlier chapters, Adam and Eve perverted the original institution of worship by an act of idolatry. That

1. Jonathan Gibson, "Worship: On Earth as It Is in Heaven," in *Reformation Worship: Liturgies from the Past for the Present*, ed. Jonathan Gibson and Mark Earngey (Greensboro, N.C.: New Growth Press, 2018), 4.

could have been the end. That act of treason could have been the doom for humanity's covenantal relationship with the Great King. But that's not what happened. Even though in Adam we failed to keep our end of the deal (faithfulness to the Lord), God maintains the covenant relationship, overcoming our sin with His abundant grace and mercy. This is why we find that as Scripture unfolds the story of God's covenant with His people, two elements are added to the original call—response—meal structure.

The first is an element of *cleansing.* Before sin entered the picture, this was unnecessary. Now, however, we are unable to answer God's initial call. We are unrighteous, unclean, and impure. We lack the holiness needed to stand before the presence of God (Heb. 12:14). Cue the sacrifices. Before the fall, worship was a bloodless affair. Ever since, God's covenantal dealings require bloodshed as a sign of atonement, as a symbol that the price of sin has been paid: "Without shedding of blood there is no remission [of sins]" (Heb. 9:22). Therefore, sacrifices became an integral part of worship for the people of God under the old covenant. To enter into a sacred meeting—a covenantal conversation—with God, the people must first be cleansed.

A second element added to the original liturgy is *commissioning* or *sending.* The communion feast is no longer the culmination of covenantal worship as it would have been in Eden. Now the meal of worship (Passover and peace offering in the old covenant, the Lord's Supper in the new covenant) would stand in as a representation of the end. Worshipers must wait in faith until the new heavens and the new earth, when we will feast with God at the marriage supper of the Lamb, for the enjoyment of what was first offered in Eden. And until that time God commissions His people with work to do. Fittingly, it is the work of gathering more worshipers.

In the old covenant, God's desire was that the world would see His covenantal relationship with Israel and come to know Him in the same way. He saved Israel so "that all the peoples of the earth may know the hand of the LORD, that it is mighty, that you may fear the LORD your God forever" (Josh. 4:24). Moreover, Israel was saved to serve God so that other nations would marvel at their wisdom and blessing (Deut. 4:6). While the covenant community had a unique relationship with

God, they were always open for more worshipers. So God would bless His people and charge them to go in His strength to accomplish this evangelistic mission, to "declare His glory among the nations, His wonders among all peoples" (1 Chron. 16:24).

So this is the basic shape of the covenant relationship that God has with His people as it is expressed in worship. God calls His people to the task of glorifying and praising Him. He then cleanses them, making them fit to receive His word and truly be consecrated, or set apart, as those who respond in faith and obedience. God shares a meal with His people as a symbol of their communion. Finally, He blesses them and sends them out into the world to declare His glory to all people.

Covenant Renewal

As you read the Old Testament, what is truly astounding is that even though God's people continued to sin again and again, failing in their charge before the Lord and consistently breaking covenant, God never cast them out. Yes, because of their sin they were kicked out (for a time) of the covenant land, but they were never kicked out of the blessed covenantal relationship that they had with Him. Instead, what we see is the God who comes to His sinful and wayward people over and over again and renews His covenantal relationship. It is almost as though Israel's persistent sin could not keep up with their Lord's persistent grace.

Consider the story of Israel's rescue from Egypt and the covenantal ceremony that took place in Exodus 19–24. There we see, first, that God *calls* the people. He brings them to Mount Sinai. This is true even back in chapters 3 and 4 when we first learned of God's plan to bring (or call) His people out of Egypt. Why is He determined to save them? That they might worship Him (4:23)! So God calls them out of a place, and He calls them into a new place—namely, Mount Sinai—where He will establish His covenant. And He gets the first word: "And God spoke all these words, saying…" (20:1).

And immediately, what does God do? He *cleanses* His people: "I am the LORD your God, who brought you out of the land of Egypt, out of the house of bondage" (Ex. 20:2). How is this a cleansing? It sounds like He's just rehearsing history for them. This is true, but it's a *redemptive* history. It's about how they were in slavery, and were it not for God's intervention they would still be in subjection to the tyranny of Egypt. Recall how the blood of the lamb spared the Israelites as the angel of death swept through the land and took Egypt's firstborn sons. Those who didn't have the blood were claimed for death; those who had the blood were cleansed for God.

So in other words, this rehearsal of God's redemptive work was a reminder that if it were not for His initiation and enabling, the Israelites would have had no hope of entering into a covenant with the Great King. He called them and made them capable of answering that call. This cleansing aspect was crucial before any other aspect of the covenantal conversation could go forward. But once God had declared them right before Him, He moved to the next phase: *consecrating*. He gave them His word (specifically, the Ten Commandments), which the people were to respond to in faith and obedience. The people lent their voice to this covenantal conversation by boldly responding, "All the words which the LORD has said we will do" (Ex. 24:3). In essence, they declare that they will be set apart from all other idols and serve God alone.

Moving toward the conclusion of the covenantal interchange, there is a meal—the people *commune* with God: "Then Moses went up, also Aaron, Nadab, and Abihu, and seventy of the elders of Israel, and they saw the God of Israel. And there was under His feet as it were a paved work of sapphire stone, and it was like the very heavens in its clarity. But on the nobles of the children of Israel He did not lay His hand. So they saw God, and they ate and drank" (Ex. 24:9–11). This is always what a proper covenantal relationship with God leads to: communion with Him. What a blessing, joy, and privilege! The people have been called by the Creator God of the universe into a personal, intimate, and life-giving relationship with Him. What could be better than that? Surely He is worthy of the worship that He commands.

You know where the story goes, though. Only a few chapters later we read the tragic tale of that infamous act of idolatry: the same people who swore their allegiance to God alone in Exodus 24 ("All these things we will do") are bowing before golden statues of cows in Exodus 32: "This is your god, O Israel, that brought you out of the land of Egypt!" (v. 4). I would think that would be the end, wouldn't you? But it's not. Amazingly God does the whole thing all over again. And again.

And again. He comes to Israel and renews with them the very covenant they broke.

So this same basic pattern occurs numerous times in the Old Testament. In Leviticus 9 Aaron leads the people of God in a worship service with this shape. We find the same in 2 Chronicles 29:20–36, where Hezekiah restores the worship that had been perverted and lost since the time of Aaron. In both passages the priest first must present to God a sin offering to atone for the guilt of the people; second, a burnt offering went up to please God and consecrate the people to Him; and last, there was a peace offering, which entailed feasting over the fellowship that the people had with God by means of the sacrifices just offered. In his book *Immanuel in Our Place: Seeing Christ in Israel's Worship*, Tremper Longman III explains the simple logic that these offerings required: namely, that a sin offering must come before a gift or peace offering. Cleansing must come before communion.[2] Again, the (multiday) worship service at the dedication of Solomon's temple in 2 Chronicles 5–7 contains gathering and calling (5:2–3), sacrifice and cleansing (5:4–6), teaching and consecration (6:1–11), feasting and communion (7:8–9), and a sending (7:10).[3]

In all these instances, God was renewing His relationship with a people who didn't deserve it. Israel could easily think, "We have sinned so greatly—there is no way God would welcome us back!" Or, "It has been so long since we have worshiped properly. Surely God has abandoned us by now." But instead, in the worship service God gives His people the very proof that He has not left them. He shows that His faithfulness never comes to an end and that His mercy is new every morning.

Covenant Redeemer

We are forced to ask at this point, But why? Why does God not give His people over because of their consistent rebellion? Why does He continue to maintain His end of the bargain even though they have failed on their end time and time again, world without end? Why does He continue to show them grace upon grace?

---

2. See Tremper Longman III, *Immanuel in Our Place: Seeing Christ in Israel's Worship* (Phillipsburg, N.J.: P&R, 2001), 77–115.

3. See Gibson, "Worship: On Earth as It Is in Heaven," 7–8.

The answer, of course, is Jesus Christ. The sin and stubbornness of the people doesn't annul the covenant because the plan was always for God to keep it. God continually came back because He knew the things that He required from Israel would one day be accomplished to perfection by Him in the person of His incarnated Son. Christ stands at the center of every covenantal conversation God has ever entered into with His people. The reason God can renew the covenant is because of the Redeemer of the covenant.

We get the first glimpse of this truth immediately after the fall. When God entered into a covenant of grace with Adam immediately after the fall, it was because of Christ. Genesis 3:15 predicts that the coming Messiah would defeat the one who stole God's worship and formed a treasonous counter-covenant with God's children. Christ is that Messiah who is the content of God's covenant promise. And all God's subsequent covenantal dealings with His people pointed to the coming of His Son.

This is the link between all the old covenant worship and our worship today. Perhaps you were wondering what relevance any of this "covenant" jargon has. Maybe your eyes were starting to glaze over as you read about old kings and dead animals. But this stuff is extremely important for understanding worship. Why? Because the worship service is where God renews the covenant that we have broken just as He once did for ancient Israel.

Did you know that? Do you recognize you are still in a covenant with God today? *Covenant* is not a term that has expired with the close of the Old Testament. We are living in the glorious time of the *new* covenant, which is marked by the ministry of the Lord Jesus Christ. But this doesn't mean that every aspect of the old covenant has been made obsolete.

Consider again this important passage from Hebrews 12. The author compares worship under the old and new covenants. He writes, "For you have not come to the mountain that may be touched and that burned with fire, and to blackness and darkness and tempest, and the sound of a trumpet and the voice of words, so that those who heard it begged that the word should not be spoken to them anymore" (vv. 18–19). This is a reference to Mount Sinai, which represents the entirety of the old covenant. We are not worshiping in the same manner as that, Hebrews tells us: "But you have come to Mount Zion and to the city of the living God, the heavenly Jerusalem... [and] to Jesus the Mediator of the new covenant" (vv. 22, 24). So Jesus does not abolish the covenantal nature of God's dealing with His people. Rather, He fulfills the covenantal nature of God's dealing with His people. Or in other words, while our covenantal worship might look different today, our worship is still covenantal. It is still about God calling us into a relationship with Him, requiring our response of faith and obedience, and promising us life and salvation.

Because Jesus did not abolish the covenant, it makes sense that the basic shape and structure of covenantal dealings and relationships with God (call—cleansing—consecrating—communion—commissioning) would still remain today. In Christian worship we go through these same motions because God is still renewing His covenant faithfulness to us in Jesus Christ. That is not to say that God's faithfulness needs to be renewed like a phone battery needs to be recharged. But as we have done so much that would warrant being rejected permanently by Him, *for our benefit* He shows to us through the worship service that His faithfulness has never run out. While we are faithless, He always remains faithful. That is what is happening in worship: God displays His covenantal faithfulness. Is it a time for us to renew our commitment and obedience to the Lord? Absolutely. But even more than that, it's a time to revel in God's unfailing commitment to us in His Son.

So consider how that basic covenantal pattern of worship is now transformed for us because of Jesus. We are now called to worship God in the name of the Son (John 14:6). We are cleansed not by anything our hands have done, not by any sacrifices we offer, but by the once-for-all sacrifice of Christ on the cross (Heb. 7:27). We are consecrated as God's people by the preaching of Christ's gospel (John 1:1; Col. 1:28; Heb. 4:12). We commune with God as we partake of the body and blood of His Son (1 Cor. 10:16). And finally, we are commissioned to serve God in the name of Christ, as those who bear the name Christian. We leave with His blessing; we serve in His strength: "Now may our Lord Jesus Christ Himself, and our God and Father, who has loved us and given us everlasting consolation and good hope by grace, comfort your hearts and establish you in every good word and work" (2 Thess. 2:16–17).

Covenant Response

You see how all these components, while still integral to what it means to worship God covenantally, have been radically changed because of Christ. Through every step of the worship service we are drawn back to the reality of worship: being conformed to the image of the invisible God through Christ (Col. 1:15; 3:10). Everything is about being recast in the story. We aren't in Adam and his idolatrous transgression anymore; we are in Christ. We aren't mere sinners any longer; we are saints—and this is a time for that identity to be stamped on our hearts.

What is our response to this wonderful work that goes on in worship? It is praise. That is our part in the covenant conversation. We praise God that although we deserve condemnation, He continually calls us back and proves His unfailing faithfulness in Jesus Christ. Paul captures this succinctly in 2 Corinthians 1:20: "For all the promises of God find their Yes in him. That is why it is through him that we utter our Amen to God for his glory" (ESV). As we established at the start of the chapter, a covenant is a relationship that is founded on promises. Here, Paul tells us that all God's promises are true and never broken—that is, are always "Yes"—because of Jesus Christ. Everything God has promised for us has come true because of the work of Jesus Christ. Then Paul tells us what our proper response to God is because of this: "Amen," or "Let it be!" It's such a tiny word, but *amen* encapsulates within it the praise, thanksgiving, and glory that we are called to give back to God in worship. So we utter, we speak, we respond with a declaration that God has done wondrous things through Jesus Christ.

Notice how according to Paul God says yes to us in Jesus and we say amen to Him also through Jesus. One commentator writes, "Christ is the 'go-between.' God speaks to us in Christ and we, who have received the message, speak back to God through Christ. The apostle is teaching us that we may approach God by no other path and glorify him by no other means. Sin prevents us approaching God in our own right; but we may draw near through Christ."[4] Jesus truly stands at the center of this covenantal conversation of worship; He is "the centre of New

---

4. Paul W. Barnett, *The Message of 2 Corinthians*, The Bible Speaks Today (Downers Grove, Ill.: InterVarsity, 1988), 39.

Testament thinking about worship. He is the ultimate meeting point between heaven and earth."[5] It is all about Him. We rehearse, as it were, again and again each week the covenant faithfulness of God to us in His Son. We rehearse the gospel, which teaches us that "there is one God and one Mediator between God and men, the Man Christ Jesus" (1 Tim. 2:5).

What a wonderful thing it is to have a mediator! It is because of Christ that we are capable of responding to God. Otherwise, when God calls us we would run and hide. The sins of thought, word, and deed we committed throughout the week convince us we could not come before the presence of God. Our sin tells us that we are too unworthy to speak back to God. We have broken covenant too many times for Him to want us any longer. But we don't come to God in our sin or in our failings. We do not "utter our Amen" through our own merits. We come through Christ.

So run to worship, dear friend. Don't hide in shame or disgrace, thinking your sin is too great for a meeting with God. He knows your sin, and He is ready to cover it with His grace. He knows you have broken covenant, but He is ready to renew it. Experience that wonder of God's never-failing faithfulness every week in worship. And with joy and thanksgiving lift your voice and respond with the covenant people: "Blessed be the LORD forevermore! Amen and Amen" (Ps. 89:52).

---

5. Peterson, *Engaging with God*, 285.

Discussion Questions

1. Why is the idea of covenant so important for understanding what happens when we worship? Why is it still important for us today, living in the light of the New Testament?

2. What are the three elements that made up the original pattern of worship before the fall, and what two elements were added after?

3. Why is cleansing a necessity in worship now?

4. Why does God continually renew His covenant with us, even though we keep breaking it?

5. What is the appropriate response from us in this covenantal conversation that we have with God in worship?

Chapter 6

We Submit to God's Agenda

Religion was never designed
To make our pleasures less.
—Isaac Watts

A serious problem in the church today is people assuming that God is akin to some fluffy puppy that we can cuddle up next to and do whatever we want with. C. S. Lewis was much closer to the mark when he portrayed God as a mighty lion in his series The Chronicles of Narnia. On hearing that the king of Narnia is a lion, the Penvensie children ask, "Is he quite safe?" The reply comes: "Who said anything about safe? 'Course he isn't safe. But he's good."

Meeting with God in worship is like coming face-to-face with a lion. It's not a safe encounter by any stretch of the imagination. It's downright dangerous. Perhaps if we had that picture in mind we wouldn't stroll into worship gatherings with such frivolity or superficiality. Perhaps we would be less prone to worship thoughtlessly or nonchalantly. If we remembered that we were coming before a powerful and unpredictable lion, we would likely heed the ancient wisdom to guard our steps when we go to the house of God (Eccl. 5:1).

But, as Aslan reminds us, while God is unsafe, He is also abundantly good. We saw that in the last chapter: as He comes to us again and again in the work of Christ, we need not be terrified to enter His presence. Furthermore, we have every reason to believe that if we heed His commands, it will go well with us as we meet with God and enter into a covenantal conversation with Him.

The Trouble with Submission

"I don't wanna!" This is the cry not just of a stubborn child but of our generation as a whole. We live in an increasingly me-centered society. Nothing is more sacred than the self, according to the prevailing message of our culture. People don't like to be told what to do. We want to follow our own course. This mentality has taken over the average church service as well. Rather than looking into God's Word to see how we ought to worship Him, we come up with our own methods based on personal preference. "Gone is any conviction that one liturgy is better than another because it conforms to revealed truth and the order of creation," laments historian D. G. Hart. "Or that one order of worship is more appropriate than another for the theology that a congregation or denomination confesses. Worship, like food or clothes, is merely a matter of taste."[1]

But if it's true that in worship we are meeting with God (and it is true), then that means God runs the meeting. After all, He is God and we are not. This is the simple argumentation used in Ecclesiastes when we are told to watch our mouths when we enter the house of God: "Do not be rash with your mouth, and let not your heart utter anything hastily before God, for God is in heaven and you on earth; therefore let your words be few" (Eccl. 5:2).

Because God is in heaven and we are on earth, we come to hear from Him. We come to do His bidding. If your boss calls you into his or her office for a one-on-one meeting, you're not going to strut in, kick your feet up on the desk, and proceed to pontificate on whatever matters you think are important. No—you've been summoned by your superior. As the inferior you sit and listen. How much more true is this when we have been summoned by *the* Superior, God Himself! We are dust and ashes before Him. If He wants an appointment with us, He will also set the agenda.

This means that worship can't look like anything we want it to look like. We can't do whatever we wish. We have to do what God wants, and He cares very much about how He is worshiped. He has high standards. Since religion and worship are very personal, people balk at the

---

1. Hart, *Recovering Mother Kirk*, 83–84.

idea that we can't do whatever we personally please. But Scripture presents the activity of worship as something much more serious and far less flippant or subjective. In fact, in some cases, worship is a matter of life or death. This is why at the beginning of chapter 5, the Preacher of Ecclesiastes says we are to "walk prudently" (ESV) as we come into the presence of God. This is not a "mind the gap" kind of step-watching; it's referring to our conduct. He is warning the people of God, "Be careful how you worship." Worship is a serious business—he uses the word "guard," hinting at potential danger. The potential danger is God's potency and power! God cares how we worship, and if we do not worship Him appropriately, we place ourselves in danger.

Now maybe that doesn't sound quite right or sit well with you. You may be thinking, *Surely God doesn't care how we worship; He simply cares* that *we worship.* For many of us, our default setting is to think that as long as our heart is in it, God is happy with our worship. But there is arrogance in that way of thinking. It places us above God. It suggests something like this: "I am so great and important that God should be thrilled at the prospect of getting any of my attention. What a privilege for Him that I would worship Him! Surely He's so attention starved that He'll take whatever I give Him."

But that's not the case. God doesn't need us. He doesn't need our worship. But if we are going to worship, we better do it properly.

God Cares How We Worship

Two stories about two brothers prove the point that God cares about how we worship. The first is in Genesis 4, and the brothers are Cain and Abel. The scene is one of worship: the two brothers are bringing their offerings to the Lord: "In the process of time it came to pass that Cain brought an offering of the fruit of the ground to the LORD. Abel also brought of the firstborn of his flock and of their fat. And the LORD respected Abel and his offering, but He did not respect Cain and his offering. And Cain was very angry, and his countenance fell" (Gen. 4:3–5). The point here is not to get into a debate about what made one offering acceptable over the other, what made one form of worship acceptable over the other. The point is simply that there is a type of worship that is acceptable and a type that is not. So we must be careful in how we worship God, for if we come to worship in an unacceptable manner, we will be disrespected by God. Did you notice that? It's not just that Cain's worship was disrespected or rejected. *He* was disregarded by God: "[God] did not respect Cain and his offering." Worship carefully.

God is the one who determines what our worship looks like. If we worship in a way that displeases Him, we, along with our worship, will be rejected. If we leave worship up to ourselves, then we will fashion it into something that we like, something that makes sense to us. The problem is that we are sinful creatures who will end up worshiping ourselves rather than God. Left to our own wisdom, at the very best we can only come up with a worship that would seem fitting for some kind of bigger, better version of ourselves. But God is not a bigger or better version of us. He's God, so therefore He calls the shots. As we will soon see, these "shots" are called in Scripture. And if we cannot find evidence in the Bible for the way we worship, that means we are worshiping in an inappropriate manner and something needs to change.

The most basic proof for this is the second commandment, "You shall not make for yourself a carved image" (Ex. 20:4), which the Westminster Larger Catechism 109 explicates to say, "The sins forbidden in the second commandment are all devising, counseling, commanding, using, anywise approving any religious worship not instituted by God himself." In the Old Testament, Nadab and Abihu—priests of Israel—learned this the hard way. This is the second story of two brothers: "Nadab and Abihu, the sons of Aaron, each took his censer and put fire in it, put incense on it, and offered profane fire before the LORD, which He had not commanded them. So fire went out from before the LORD and devoured them, and they died before the LORD" (Lev. 10:1–2). They came to God with "profane" (the Hebrew word here means "strange" or "forbidden") fire. Again, we are not concerned here with what exactly that meant. The point is simply that there was a type of offering, or worship, that was authorized and there was a type that wasn't. God cares about how we worship—so much so that He took the lives of these two people who worshiped Him in an inappropriate—and strictly forbidden (Ex. 30:1)—manner! In response to this event God says,

> By those who come near Me
> I must be regarded as holy;

> And before all the people
> I must be glorified. (Lev. 10:3)

He will be "regarded as holy" among the people who draw near to Him in worship—either by faith or by fire from heaven.

If that isn't the clearest evidence that God cares how we worship and that God alone tells us how we may worship, then I don't know what else is. We see how seriously God takes worship, and therefore we should take it seriously too. In a tract titled *The Necessity of Reforming the Church*, John Calvin wrote:

> There is a two-fold reason why the Lord, in condemning and prohibiting all fictitious worship, requires us to give obedience only to his own voice. First, it tends greatly to establish his authority that we do not follow our own pleasure, but depend entirely on his sovereignty; and secondly, such is our folly, that when we are left at liberty, all we are able to do is go astray. And then once we have turned aside from the right path, there is no end to our wanderings, until we get buried under a multitude of superstitions. Justly, therefore, does the Lord, in order to assert his full right of dominion, strictly enjoin what he wishes us to do, and at once reject all human devices which are at variance with his command. Justly, too, does he, in express terms, define our limits, that we may not, by fabricating perverse modes of worship, provoke his anger against us.[2]

This teaches us that worship must be a God-ward activity, and never human-ward. If we aim at ourselves and our wants, as Calvin says, we are going to be led astray on a trail that takes us to our destruction. Terry Johnson says that "there are only two options in worship. It can be people-centered or God-centered. It cannot be both."[3] He goes on to ask, "What can we do to move our worship services in a God-centered direction? The single most important step is to fill them with biblical content. Bible-filled services, services in which the songs, prayers, readings, and sermons are full of Scripture, will inevitably be filled with God

---

2. John Calvin, *The Necessity of Reforming the Church*, trans. H. Beveridge (Dallas: Protestant Heritage Press, 1995), 17.

3. Johnson, *Worshipping with Calvin*, 66.

as well."[4] This is to simply affirm what we mentioned earlier: that God calls the shots in worship.

Worshiping by the Word

What we have seen thus far is that God cares how we worship, and furthermore we know we are worshiping in a way that pleases Him when we worship according to His word. Put another way, the word of God must regulate what goes on in the corporate service. We must do those things that the Bible commands, and we must certainly never do those things that the Bible forbids (to the grim tale of Nadab and Abihu we could add Uzzah of 2 Samuel 6 as a cautionary warning!).

Those things that the Bible clearly commands and prescribes are called *elements*. Elements are the nonnegotiables; they are the scripturally mandated parts of what it means to publicly assemble and worship God. Elements of worship would include things such as gathering for preaching, praying, and partaking of the sacraments. For example, we are told that in the earliest days of the Christian church "they continued steadfastly in the apostles' doctrine and fellowship, in the breaking of bread, and in [the] prayers" (Acts 2:42). Other elements include reading Scripture (Col. 4:16; 1 Tim. 4:13; 1 Thess. 5:27; 2 Thess. 3:14), singing (1 Cor. 14:15; Eph. 5:19; Col. 3:16), giving gifts for the needs of the church and to the poor (Acts 6:1–6; Rom. 12:8, 13; 2 Cor. 8:19–21; 9:11–15), public confession of faith (1 Tim. 6:15; 2 Tim. 1:13–14; 2 Thess. 2:15), and confession of sin (1 John 1:8–10).[5]

Along with elements, *circumstances* is another helpful category to keep in mind when we consider what belongs in the worship service. Circumstances are those things not mandated in Scripture, and it requires wisdom to implement them in the right and appropriate worship of God. These include issues like what time to have the morning service, what the preacher should wear, and whether the congregation should use songbooks or projectors. Part of proper worship is recognizing what things are elements and what things are circumstances,

---

4. Johnson, *Worshipping with Calvin*, 79.
5. This list is compiled from Edmund Clowney's larger list, as cited in Carson, "Worship under the Word," in *Worship by the Book*, ed. Carson, 48.

and not to get them mixed up. Sadly, many churches spend a lot of time arguing about circumstances as though they held the authoritative place of elements. How many people have left churches over something as mundane as what color to paint the sanctuary, whether or not the church should get new carpet, or (you fill in the blank of pettiness and minutiae)?

This is not to say that circumstantial things are entirely inconsequential. God very much cares that our worship services be done "decently and in order" (1 Cor. 14:40). So Johnson reminds us, "The Apostles regularly appeal to what is 'fitting' or 'suitable' or 'proper,' in light of Scripture's explicit commands, and yet without spelling out exactly what these things mean. They expect that believers will apply wisdom and discern what is appropriate."[6]

God Serves Us

Another important consideration regarding worship is what to do with these elements. Is there a proper order in which we should arrange these things? What shape should our liturgy take? We will consider this more in depth in the following chapter, but suffice it to say that there ought to be a clear structure that presents the gospel—or, in the words of Terry Johnson, there should be a "gospel logic" to what goes on in our services: adoring God's greatness; confessing our sinfulness; hearing of forgiveness in Christ; and being built up into Christ through preaching, prayer, and sacraments. This is God's goal: that through worship we be reminded over and over again of the work that He does for us in the gospel.

Notice a significant point about worship: while it's true that the word *liturgy* refers to the work of the people, the primary work of worship is done by God Himself.[7] This is not to say that we are passive in

---

6. Terry Johnson, *Reformed Worship: Worship That Is according to Scripture* (Jackson, Miss.: Reformed Academic Press, 2010), 7. See also Eph. 5:3–4; 1 Tim. 2:9–10; and Titus 2:1 in support of Johnson's point.

7. Robert Letham writes, "We are inclined to view worship as what we do, but… it is *first and foremost* something the triune God does; our actions are initiated and encompassed by his." "The Trinity in Worship," in *The Essential Trinity: New Testament Foundations and Practical Relevance*, ed. Brandon D. Crowe and Carl R. Trueman (Phillipsburg, N.J.: P&R, 2016), 273, emphasis original.

worship—far from it. But it highlights that when we come together for worship, we are meeting to have something done to and for us. We are meeting to be changed. The workshop of worship is not one in which we are working; rather, it's one in which we are worked on. Theologian John Thompson has said, "If one understands the New Testament and the view it gives of how we meet with and know God and worship him as triune, then worship is not primarily our act but, like our salvation, is God's gift before or as it is our task."[8]

This is not to say that we primarily come to worship for what we can get out of it. Our spiritual transformation is a result of worship, not the reason for worship. The reason is God and His glory. This can never be said too much. But even so, it's important to see that corporate worship is one of the major ways that God graciously serves us. In that sense, it is appropriate that we call our Lord's Day gatherings a *service*. God serves us in grace; we serve Him in gratitude. Worship is always about us responding to what God is doing to, for, in, and through us. This is part of the way we will be properly shaped as people of God in our worship: when we recognize every week how much He does in comparison with how little we have to offer.

We should lament the recent trend in many evangelical churches to give primacy of place to music and singing. When these elements become the majority of the worship service, what are we subliminally telling ourselves? We are saying that we have more to offer to God than He has to offer to us.[9] But worship is primarily about God serving us. Think of this in comparison to the cultural liturgies that we often buy into. In world worship, the world serves us a lie. In godly worship, God serves us grace. He serves us His very self.

We Submit to Him
My firstborn is at the age when he knows that certain things are off-limits. As he scurries into my study (which is already supposed to be

---

8. As quoted in Letham, "Trinity and Worship," in *Essential Trinity*, ed. Crowe and Trueman, 274.

9. Jon D. Payne recognizes this issue in his book *In the Splendor of Holiness: Rediscovering the Beauty of Reformed Worship for the 21st Century* (White Hall, W.V.: Tolle Lege Press, 2008), 28.

off-limits), he immediately goes to play with the printer (which is even more off-limits). Yet the prohibition seems to encourage his disobedience all the more. Sometimes when he thinks I'm not watching, he will crawl over to the printer and look around to see if Mom or Dad will catch him before he proceeds.

Submission doesn't come naturally to us. Ever since the fall we all want to break free from any higher power or authority and go our own way. We want to do our own thing instead of submitting to the will of someone who is over us. While we might be able to get away with it at home with our parents, we can't get away with it at church with our heavenly Father. God is the highest authority of all, and a fundamental aspect of attributing this power and glory to Him is to do as He commands. Hopefully all Christians would agree that we must submit to what God commands for us in life. But for some reason, when it comes to Sunday worship things are different. We fall back into that "I don't wanna!" mentality. But if we are to obey God throughout the week, that obedience rightly starts at the opening of the week in earnest and honest worship.

Corporate worship is a time when we come together and God audibly, through the ministry of the word, reminds us of the important reality that He is king and we are His subjects. He is Lord, and we are servants. He is shepherd, and we are sheep. He is God, and we are His creatures—"God is in heaven, and you on earth" (Eccl. 5:2). So we must do what He says. Since submission doesn't come naturally to us, we need to learn it. It isn't easy, so we need to work at it. Worship is where we learn and are trained in the disciplines that are crucial to the Christian life: trust, obedience, submission—or, in a word, faith. "Worship is…faith expressing itself in obedience and adoration."[10] The God-centered worship service is the garden in which faith is planted, grown, and cultivated.

We therefore must surrender our wants and preferences and recognize that whatever God says goes. And when we do that, we truly reflect Christ. For the Son is the one who perfectly submits to the will of the Father in all things. And as we come to corporate worship with an intention to please God over ourselves, it's a way in which we can fulfill

---

10. Peterson, *Engaging with God*, 283.

the call of the apostle Paul: that we would have the mind of Christ, being humble and taking the form of a servant before God (Phil. 2:5–8).

And why shouldn't we submit to God in worship? We have just learned that He is serving us, after all! He is doing a work that is for our everlasting good! His intention is to pour out His grace and abundantly bless us. Why wouldn't we want that? To try to devise our own methods and schemes for worshiping God is tantamount to rejecting the lifeline tossed into the water to save us as we drown.

Our prayer should always be that the Lord would align our wills and wants with His. We must always desire that the Spirit would bring us into joyful, complete, perfect harmony with the sovereign pleasure of God. So ask yourself every Sunday as you are about to enter worship: Can I say, "Not my will, but Yours be done"?

Discussion Questions

1. Why is submission so difficult for us? How does this become an issue in worship?

2. Does God care simply that we worship, or also how we worship? Give some scriptural evidence.

3. Why must the Bible be our only guide for how we worship?

4. What is the distinction between *elements* and *circumstances* in worship?

5. In what way can it be said that God serves us in the worship service?

Chapter 7

We Commune with the Saints

According to the arrangement of God, the Christian is more of a Christian in society than alone, and more in the enjoyment of privileges of a spiritual kind when he shares them with others, than when he possesses them apart.

—James Bannerman

Every aspect of our life should be lived to the glory of God. As Paul says, "Whether you eat or drink, or whatever you do, do all to the glory of God" (1 Cor. 10:31). In that sense, we could say that all of life is meant to be worship. We could say that, and many people do say that, but I think it would be more helpful to say that all of life is meant to be worship*ful*. This helps distinguish what we do in our everyday versus what we do in the Lord's house on His day with His people, which is the focus of this book. Worship must be consistent with our everyday lives, but it is distinct from them as well.

Worship finds its fullest and truest expression in the called, corporate setting. Again, this is not to take away the validity or importance of private or family worship. These are biblically commanded practices that are crucial for our spiritual formation and maturity. But as humans are wired for worship, that design finds its ultimate fulfillment when we worship *together*. God did not create one lone-ranger worshiper. Rather, He saw that it was not good for Adam to be alone, so He formed a helper suitable for Him. A helper for what, exactly? One to help Adam in his work of glorifying and enjoying God in His garden sanctuary—the very first place of worship. In Genesis 12:2 God gave a call to Abram individually, but it had a corporate scope: "I will make you a great nation." Many years later, God saved that entire nation for a distinct purpose: "that they may serve Me" (Ex. 8:1). In the midst of serious darkness and despair, Elijah's comfort came in knowing that God had spared multiple worshipers: "Yet I have reserved seven thousand in Israel, *all whose knees have not bowed to Baal*, and every mouth that has not kissed him" (1 Kings 19:18). And we see in Revelation that the full joy of heaven is not experienced by the glorified saint alone in his or her celestial prayer closet—it's experienced in thunderous worship with the myriads on myriads who have been ransomed from their sin to now join in unison singing,

> Blessing and honor and glory and power
> Be to Him who sits on the throne,
> And to the Lamb, forever and ever! (Rev. 5:13)

Thus far in this book, we've been looking at the amazing things that God is doing in and through and for us as individuals in corporate worship, but in this chapter I want to really focus on the corporate aspect. Believe it or not, there is something wonderfully supernatural that goes on when we meet with fellow believers to worship God. That is not because there is anything intrinsically spiritual about gathering as a group. Nothing supernatural goes on in an overflowing sports arena or in a crowded movie theater or in a college lecture hall just because there are a lot of people.

No, none of these compare to the work that God does through His Spirit in the lives of His corporately gathered people in worship. So let's try to recover an appreciation for what the Apostles' Creed has codified as the "communion of saints"—which "very well expresses what the church is."[1] I want to do this by exploring two things that happen when we worship together. First, we are corporately and collectively separated from the world, and second, we are united to one another.

Separated from the World

Many Christians today have forgotten that there is meant to be a fundamental distinction between the church and the world. By *world* I do

---

1. Calvin, *Institutes*, 4.1.3.

not mean this earth or all humanity, but rather the kingdom of Satan and sin. For example, this is how Paul uses the term in Romans 12:2: "Do not be conformed to this world, but be transformed by the renewing of your mind, that you may prove what is that good and acceptable and perfect will of God." The will of God is distinct from the will and desires of this world. Paul writes in Galatians 6:14, "But God forbid that I should boast except in the cross of our Lord Jesus Christ, by whom the world has been crucified to me, and I to the world." Christians are meant to be dead to the world, meaning that we are to have no living and active relationship with sin and evil.

If you asked most Christians if they are meant to be distinct from the world, I imagine their theology would cause them to agree. They would remember the words of John: "Do not love the world or the things in the world. If anyone loves the world, the love of the Father is not in him" (1 John 2:15). But when it comes to worship practices, many Christians are seemingly giving a different answer. There has been a big push in the last several decades to transform worship services into something that attracts the non-Christian. Church services resemble the experience of a movie theater, concert venue, or a cowboy rodeo (not joking) more than an encounter between God and redeemed sinners, as historically has been the case. Yet when we capitulate our worship to the trends of the culture, we have lost something powerful that is meant to be happening in worship: we are meant to be separated from the world. The worship service is the time and place where God reminds us we have been called out and set apart from the kingdom of this world and have been transferred into the kingdom of His beloved Son (Col. 1:13). How can that happen when our celebration of Christ's kingdom borrows the means and methods of the kingdom of sin? Theologian J. Gresham Machen said back in 1925, and perceptively so, that when the church loses its distinction from the world "the power of the Church is gone. The Church then becomes like salt that has lost its savor, and is fit only to be cast out and to be trodden under foot of men."[2]

The fear and objection is that if the church looks too different, people won't like us very much. This is certainly true. But according to

---

2. As quoted in Hart and Muether, *With Reverence and Awe*, 25.

Jesus, that's part of the point: "If you were of the world, the world would love its own. Yet because you are not of the world, but I chose you out of the world, therefore the world hates you" (John 15:19). We are chosen out of the world, and our worship services should reflect that. They should be, in the most literal sense of the term, *otherworldly*—they are taking place in heaven after all! This idea of being chosen by God is behind both the Hebrew and Greek words (*qahal* and *ekklēsia*) used for corporate worshiping assemblies; when we gather God wants it to be clear it's because we belong to Him, and not the world.[3]

Please do not misunderstand me: I am not saying the church is a closed-door meeting of some private and exclusive club. The church is meant to be a place for converting sinners, a place where people are transformed and rescued from the kingdom of sin. How can this happen if we bar the door to them? All people must be welcome into the church's corporate worship. But we must recognize that God is doing something in and among His people that He is not doing among unrepentant sinners. An unbeliever comes to a worship service with ignorance about who we are and who God is: "Therefore the world does not know us, because it did not know Him" (1 John 3:1). The Spirit of God is at work in the hearts of true worshipers, but not of mere observers: "And I will pray the Father, and He will give you another Helper, that He may abide with you forever—the Spirit of truth, whom the world cannot receive, because it neither sees Him nor knows Him; but you know Him, for He dwells with you and will be in you" (John 14:16–17). While the worship service is the arena of great blessing for Christians, it is also a terrifying realm of cursing for those who do not come in true faith: "Therefore whoever eats this bread or drinks this cup of the Lord in an unworthy manner will be guilty of the body and blood of the Lord" (1 Cor. 11:27).

So, yes, we gladly welcome the world into the worship service, all the while remembering that worship is not for the world. One pastor I know sometimes opens the worship service by saying, "If you are not a Christian, we are glad you are with us today. We hope you will be encouraged by your time with us. But I must warn you that we come to

---

3. We'll explore further the significance of the term *church* in the next chapter.

meet with God today, and if you are not right with Him, you may not like what He reveals to you about Himself." That's the idea. If worship is a place where we meet with God (and it is), then to meet Him apart from the mediation of Jesus Christ is a terrifying thing. That means the worship service becomes a place where the unconverted stand before the Judge in their sin, and nothing else. All they bring is their worldliness. And what a tragic thing for the church to try to woo in the world by using the gimmicks of the world—it's tantamount to luring in a fish with the very thing that will kill it!

The worship of God is not for the world—it's for God. And God is glorified in the hearts of true believers who approach Him with reverence and awe through His appointed means. One of God's appointed means is preaching, and preaching the gospel is what can make unconverted sinners right with God and bring them into the covenant community. Countless unbelievers walk into worship every Sunday. The preacher has an obligation and a burden to present to them the glories of the gospel so that through the power of the Spirit and the word they would walk out of worship converted. But if this does not happen, no matter how faithfully unbelievers may attend church, they are lacking what life is really all about: true worship.

For the unbeliever, even a churched unbeliever, worship will lack that sanctifying power and purpose. Yet this is where faithful believers are conformed to more and more look like children of heaven and less like children of this fallen world. The church service is a collective separation of the redeemed people on earth—a gathering of the remnant in an idolatrous world. How often we think, like Elijah, that sin and Satan are prevailing and we are all that's left. Yet when we come to church, it's as though God says to us, "I have reserved for Myself seven thousand men who have not bowed the knee to Baal" (Rom. 11:4).

There is strength in numbers. In worship we are drawn away from the enemy and reminded of the brothers and sisters fighting alongside us. We are drawn together to a place of refuge in a war zone. We are led together to an oasis in the desert. In worship we, as it were, step out of the realm of sin and death and darkness and enter the realm of salvation and life and light. It's the realm we belong to every moment by faith, and yet God confirms that reality to us by sight through weekly corporate worship.

United to One Another

As God reminds us that we do not belong to the world, He simultaneously is reminding us that we belong to one another. The Christian worship service is not just an opportunity for us to display to others that we are on the same team, as though we are doing nothing more than wearing the same jerseys. It's not merely a venue of our fidelity to other brothers and sisters in Christ. It is actually the means that God uses to unite us to one another. In the worship service we are drawn deeper and deeper into Christ, and therefore closer and closer to one another. Consider the following ways in which God unites His saints through the weekly gathering of worship.

United as a Body

When the Holy Spirit works faith in us and unites us to Christ, He also unites us to everyone else who is in Christ. The apostle Paul says we are so closely connected it is appropriate to consider us as being part of a body: "There is one body and one Spirit" (Eph. 4:4). Because we all have the same Spirit and the same Savior and the same Father—because we all share the same faith—we therefore belong together (vv. 5–6). That is not to say we are all the same. We certainly have different gifts and abilities. But that's why the body analogy is helpful. As Paul says in Romans, "For as we have many members in one body, but all the members do not have the same function, so we, being many, are one body in Christ, and individually members of one another" (12:4–5).

Paul essentially echoes himself in 1 Corinthians 12: "For as the body is one and has many members, but all the members of that one body, being many, are one body, so also is Christ" (v. 12). Paul compares the Christian's unique gifting with the indispensable role that each body part plays in the proper functioning of the whole. And while these gifts are to be used to glorify God throughout the entire Christian life, Paul highlights gifts that find particular expression in the context of the local church and its worship: prophecy, teaching, exhortation, and leading. This is especially clear in 1 Corinthians 12, which comes in the greater context of Paul's exhortation that the church's worship be conducted decently and in good order. And even those gifts that belong outside the realm of the worship service are still nurtured, cultivated, and strengthened inside the worship service. Thus Paul goes on in Ephesians 4:11–12 to say, "And He Himself gave some to be apostles, some prophets, some evangelists, and some pastors and teachers, for the equipping of the saints for the work of ministry, for the edifying of the body of Christ."

In either case, the point is the same. It is when the body comes together that it is built up. When we meet together for corporate worship, we are enabled to live out our Spirit-given function within the body of Christ. We are able to experience the blessing that God has for us through the hands of other believers, and we are in turn able to bless them. We are reminded that there is no such thing as a lone-ranger Christian. Not belonging to a church is tantamount to dismemberment or decapitation. God wants neither for us. Rather, He wants us to find unity in diversity, to see the multitude of gifts that He has given, but to see that they all flow from the same fount of grace: "But one and the same Spirit works all these things, distributing to each one individually as He wills" (1 Cor. 12:11). There is one grace (*charis*), but many grace gifts (*charisma*). We come to worship to give to and receive these gifts from one another. We come to be united to one another and therefore bring life to the body in its fullest. So in its chapter on the communion of the saints, the Westminster Confession of Faith 26.1 says that Christians "being united to one another in love, have communion in each other's gifts and graces, and are obliged to the performance of such duties, public and private, as do conduce to their mutual good, both in the inward and outward man."

United as a Temple

Another metaphor used in the New Testament for the corporate gathering of saints is that of a worship building, or a temple. There is some overlap with the building imagery and the body imagery, as in Ephesians 4:12, where Paul says the purpose of gifts is "for the edifying of [or, "building up" ESV] the body of Christ." Jesus Himself says that the true temple is His body (John 2:21), so we can't fully understand either of these metaphors apart from the other.

There are at least two important things to glean from what it means for the church to be a temple. First, it reminds us that the primary role of the church is indeed worship. In the old covenant, the temple was the location of worship. That is still true in the new covenant, but what has changed is that we have now become the temple: "Do you not know that you are the temple of God and that the Spirit of God dwells in you?" (1 Cor. 3:16). This teaches us that we are indispensable to the work of worship! Don't misunderstand me: this does not mean we are indispensable to God. God does not need worship, nor does He need us. But He is pleased to be worshiped, and He has chosen for that worship to take place only in and through us. What a marvel!

Have you been noticing the plural pronouns being used throughout this book? I have been fairly intentional about it, but this chapter is the perfect occasion to point it out. God has chosen for worship to be an activity in which He is glorified not only through me personally or through you personally, but through us corporately. Consider these words from Paul: "In [Him] you also are being built together for a dwelling place of God in the Spirit" (Eph. 2:22). The dwelling place—or the temple—for God, the location of His worship, takes a community. It requires more than an individual. We are not being built alone into a dwelling place; we are being built together! When we come corporately, we are transformed by the Spirit into the worship center for God's glory.

But the absence of a physical temple in the new covenant teaches us a second thing: temple imagery actually points us to the worship that is to come in the new heavens and the new earth. The world to come will be a place that is all and only and everywhere worship. John writes, therefore, "I saw no temple in it, for the Lord God Almighty and the Lamb are its temple" (Rev. 21:22). The ubiquity of God with His people in the new Jerusalem means there is no need for a specific worship center. He will dwell with us, and we will dwell with Him, and our every breath, thought, and action will be one of unadulterated worship. But we do not need to wait until the consummation to experience that glory—we get a glimpse of it in the here and now every time we come together for corporate worship. In church God stamps on us our identity as being the building blocks of that world to come. We belong to something that is not going to pass away. We have begun our eternal and heavenly work here on earth. The Spirit is uniting us now and building us up now in worship for that grand, never-ending service of worship in glory. So, Peter writes, "you also, as living stones, are being built up a spiritual house, a holy priesthood, to offer up spiritual sacrifices acceptable to God through Jesus Christ" (1 Peter 2:5). For what purpose are we being united to one another? "To offer up spiritual sacrifices acceptable to God." In a word, to worship.

United across Space and Time
Two essential attributes of God are His *immensity* and *infinity*. Immensity refers to God's presence everywhere, sometimes called His omnipresence. He fills all space. There is no nook or cranny where God is not found. Infinity teaches the same truth but in regard to time: there is no point in time in which God is not present. This is God's eternality. This means that when the immense and infinite Holy Spirit fills us we are united to all other Christians, no matter where they are and no matter when they were.

Amazing.

Have you ever had the experience of worshiping in a foreign country? If you can't speak the language used in the service, it can be a fairly bizarre experience. The few times I have had this privilege, I always perk up when I hear a familiar word: the inevitable "amen," a sung "hallelujah," or some names from Scripture. But the more stirring moments have been when I recognize something *not* in my language: the distinguishable cadence of the Lord's Prayer or the Apostles' Creed, for instance. Or the familiar tune of the Doxology or the Gloria Patri. Hearing these traditional Christian creeds and hymns said or sung in an unfamiliar language sent chills down my spine. Why? Because it was a powerful reminder of the space-defying unity of the church—or, in more technical terms, what is commonly called the catholicity or universality of the church. Indeed, the true church can be found all over the world!

When we worship, the Spirit not only lifts our souls to heaven but also acts as a tether that binds all faithful worshipers across land and sea, language and ethnicity, denominations and diversities. When we recite something like the Apostles' Creed, what a wonderful thing it is to remember that there are believers in Uganda, Bolivia, Australia, Cambodia, and China confessing the very same faith! Every Lord's Day, worship halls around the globe are flooded with the praises and prayers of the saints, who are united in the one Spirit, through the mediation of the one Son, giving thanks to the one Father. Paul says that we are "saints, with all who in every place call on the name of Jesus Christ our Lord" (1 Cor. 1:2). Later on in the book he writes about how the Corinthians "in the name of our Lord Jesus Christ…are gathered together, along with my spirit" (5:4). Paul believed that he didn't need to be in the same location as this congregation to be truly present with them.

Even more breathtaking than uniting us with believers wherever they are is that worship also unites believers whenever they are. This is commonly referred to as the *invisible church*, which the Westminster divines define as "the whole number of the elect, that have been, are, or shall be gathered into one, under Christ the Head thereof" (WCF 25.1). We have already discussed in chapter 4 the ways in which we worship with the saints who have gone on before us into heaven (Heb. 12:23). Let me point out that this is another beautiful thing about using ancient creeds and songs: it's a way of locking hands, so to speak, with the glorified saints with whom we are spiritually and mystically united. We must resist the culture's push for *new, new, new*. Rather, the church should "show her age." Jonathan Gibson and Mark Earngey write,

> Any church that cuts itself loose from the stream of Christian worship throughout history is a church that risks severing itself from her heritage, and from her Head. For Christ is Lord of the Church's history and heritage; he is Head of his body, the Church—a Church formed, not in the last six years, but over the last six millennia, since God first spoke his formative word of grace in the Garden of Eden (Gen. 3:15). Thus, when the Church gathers for worship today, she ought to reveal her ancient roots.[4]

---

4. Gibson and Earngey, *Reformation Worship*, 50–51.

Similarly, as we keep our worship pure and true and faithful to the Bible, we lay the foundation for a future generation of worshipers— God-honoring worship is a means of "guard[ing] the good deposit" entrusted to us (2 Tim. 1:14 ESV).

Did you realize that all this was going on in corporate worship? Did you ever think it could legitimately be said that in worship we actually do a bit of time travel? Did you know you are being transported through cosmic dimensions and by faith placed in heaven?

I bet there's nothing else in your week that could ever top that.

Discussion Questions

1. Why is corporate worship so important? What places in Scripture show that God has always been concerned with having a people worship Him rather than just an individual?

2. In what ways does worship separate us from the world?

3. How does the term *church* speak to our separation from the world?

4. In what ways does worship unite us with believers?

5. How does the knowledge that you are worshiping with saints all over the universe and in time affect the way you think about church?

PART 2:
The Anatomy of a Worship Service

Chapter 8

God Calls Us

True worship serves above all else the praise of God's glory.
—Hughes Oliphant Old

Having explored some general but foundational principles about the supernatural wonder behind Christian worship (meeting with God, being conformed to His image, communing with the saints, rehearsing the gospel, and renewing God's covenant faithfulness to us), in the next few chapters we want to narrow our focus. We are going to be examining each main aspect of the covenantal conversation we have with God when we come into His presence in worship. We will not only give particular attention to how these aspects together form the gospel story of God's covenant faithfulness in Christ but also see how they individually tell that story and impress it on our hearts. Terry Johnson is right when he says that "we relive the gospel every time we gather as a church to worship.... Consequently, a proper service of worship centers on Christ, and each element, from praise to confession to intercession to Scripture reading and preaching focuses on the benefits which flow from the cross."[1]

This gospel story of worship fittingly begins with the call to worship. In this portion of the liturgy, we learn that *God calls us to the most important work imaginable, hears our plea for help, and promises to be with us and accept us despite our inadequacies.*

---

1. Johnson, *Worshipping with Calvin*, 223.

The Power of the Word

Why does the worship service begin with a call? More specifically, why does it begin with God's call? It all has to do with the power of the word of God. Our God is a God of the word. He is a God who speaks. Not only that, He is a God who speaks and in doing so accomplishes great things. Yes, God is also a God of visions and dreams and wonders, but He is primarily a God who uses the spoken word. He emphasizes the role of speech time and time again. This can be seen from the beginning of Scripture.

In the opening chapters of Genesis alone, we see a multitude of ways in which God uses the spoken word. Most notably, God speaks the world into creation: "Then God said, 'Let there be light'; and there was light" (Gen. 1:3). God's word has *power*, but it also has *authority*, seen in the instructions and commission given to humankind in subsequent verses. Moreover, His word has the ability to *impart blessing and life*: "Then God blessed them, and God said to them, 'Be fruitful and multiply; fill the earth and subdue it; have dominion over the fish of the sea, over the birds of the air, and over every living thing that moves on the earth'" (v. 28). In Genesis 3:15 we find the terrifying inverse: God speaks *curse* on His rebellious creatures. His word is able to bring pain and toil and, most importantly, pronounce the definitive end to the work of Satan.

As we move through Scripture, we find that God does more than create, bless, and curse by His word. He also *communicates* with His people. It was through the spoken word that God entered into relationships with the most essential characters in redemptive history. He called Abram, He commissioned Moses, He covenanted with David all by speech (Gen. 12:1; Ex. 3:4; 2 Sam. 7:5–16). He called to service the great prophets Samuel and Jeremiah—even Jonah—through the means of His word. In the instance of Jeremiah, we have a clear example of the covenantal conversation that goes on when God calls us:

> Then the word of the LORD came to me, saying,
>> "Before I formed you in the womb I knew you,
>> Before you were born I sanctified you;
>> I ordained you a prophet to the nations."

Then said I,
  "Ah, Lord GOD!
  Behold, I cannot speak, for I am a youth."
But the LORD said to me:
  "Do not say, 'I am a youth';
  For you shall go to all to whom I send you,
  And whatever I command you, you shall speak.
  Do not be afraid of their faces,
  For I am with you to deliver you," says the LORD. (Jer. 1:4–8)

As Rayburn points out, "God speaks first, and the prophet answered with a confession of his inability. God speaks again, reassuring the prophet with the promise of His presence."[2] God calls Jeremiah, subsequently cleansing him so that he might be fit to accomplish the task given to him.

More than *constituting* the relationship between God and His people, the word of God also served as the *content* of that relationship. For in God's word is bound up all His promises, decrees, commands, and comforts. Israel's covenant with the Lord began at Sinai, where God audibly spoke to Moses all His commands. These were then canonized in written form, and the word became the foundation of the people's way of life. It was this word that they were to write on their hearts (Deut. 6:6). It was this word that they were to meditate on day and night (Ps. 1:2). It was this word that would be their way of life (Deut. 30:16).

The Divine Initiator

So then why is God's word the proper place to begin worship? Because it's God's word, not man's, that has the power to constitute a relationship with Him. If we are to come and engage with Him—which is what is happening in worship—then He needs to call us. The Westminster divines explain, "The distance between God and the creature is so great, that although reasonable creatures do owe obedience unto Him as their Creator, yet they could never have any fruition of Him as their blessedness and reward, but by some voluntary condescension on God's part"

2. Rayburn, *O Come, Let Us Worship*, 120.

(WCF 7.1). He is too great for us to grasp, lest He make Himself available to us.

We could also think of it this way: only God has the power to bring something out of nothing. That's what He did in creation, that's what He does in redemption, and that's what He is doing in worship. Think of creation: when we were absolutely nothing, God, by the power of His word, called us into existence: "Let Us make man in Our image" (Gen. 1:26). We didn't will ourselves into existence—God did. And just as He brought us out of the dark void of Genesis 1:2, He brings us out of the dark void of sin in redemption: "Most assuredly, I say to you, the hour is coming, and now is, when the dead will hear the voice of the Son of God; and those who hear will live" (John 5:25). "To him the doorkeeper opens, and the sheep hear his voice; and he calls his own sheep by name and leads them out" (John 10:3). "You did not choose Me, but I chose you and appointed you that you should go and bear fruit, and that your fruit should remain, that whatever you ask the Father in My name He may give you" (John 15:16).[3]

In these texts we see that God is always the initiator. Paul makes this point in Galatians 4:9, as though he wants to correct any errant thinking about who starts and sustains the relationship, regardless of our common parlance: "But now after you have known God, or rather are known by God, how is it that you turn again to the weak and beggarly elements, to which you desire again to be in bondage?" Paul makes an explicit connection between God's calling in creation and His calling in redemption in 2 Corinthians 4:6: "For it is the God who commanded light to shine out of darkness, who has shone in our hearts to give the light of the knowledge of the glory of God in the face of Jesus Christ."

Just as God calls us in creation and in redemption, He also calls us to the greatest work His redeemed people could ever take up in the created world: worship. The word *church* in the Greek is *ekklesia*, which means "called out ones" or "summoned ones." In our very name, we recognize that we are those whose entire identity hangs on the fact that we are in a relationship with God in which He is *calling* us.

---

3. See also Gen. 15:7–8; Deut. 7:7–8; Mark 1:17; Rom. 8:28–30; Eph. 1:3–6; 2:1–7; 4:1; 2 Thess. 2:13; 2 Tim. 1:9; 1 Peter 1:3.

Calling us from what, from where? Calling us to what, to where? As we saw in the previous chapter, God is calling us from the worthlessness of the world—where we have been for the past six days—and into His worthy presence, where a single day is better than a thousand elsewhere (Ps. 84:10). This one day in seven will reorient us, reshape us, put the imprint of the gospel story on our hearts, and erase all the false impressions that the world has left on us about what the good life really is. Truly, just as in creation and redemption, we could say that in worship we are called out of nothing and into something—life itself.

The call to worship is not just a way to begin the service; it's not even a way to reorient our minds to thinking of God, though it should do that. It is preeminently God through the minister calling His people into a covenantal relationship, a covenantal conversation. To say that the call to worship is anything less is to make a massive understatement of what is happening when we worship. When we worship God calls us—He demands that we enter into His presence and have dealings with Him.

And for what purpose? To give Him the honor that is due His name. This is what we find so frequently in old covenant worship, especially in the Psalms; God would speak to His people through the worship leader to command them to bring Him praise, honor, and glory. Psalm 100 is a classic example:

Make a joyful shout to the LORD, all you lands!
Serve the LORD with gladness;
Come before His presence with singing.
Know that the LORD, He is God;
It is He who has made us, and not we ourselves;
We are His people and the sheep of His pasture.

Enter into His gates with thanksgiving,
And into His courts with praise.
Be thankful to Him, and bless His name.
For the LORD is good;
His mercy is everlasting,
And His truth endures to all generations.

Notice the covenantal structure of this call: it begins with a command from God to worship Him, but it doesn't leave us wondering why we should. It also gives us the reasons for worship. He is our creator and our shepherd; He is good, merciful, and faithful. These attributes, characteristics, and redemptive-historical facts are meant to stir up a response in us to praise.

That's why even a call-to-worship text that doesn't have an explicit command to sing or to praise or to worship but has an explicit description of who God is still carries with it an implicit command to worship. For example, consider these words from the apostle Paul:

> Oh, the depth of the riches both of the wisdom and knowledge of God! How unsearchable are His judgments and His ways past finding out!
> "For who has known the mind of the LORD?
> Or who has become His counselor?"
> "Or who has first given to Him
> And it shall be repaid to him?"
> For of Him and through Him and to Him are all things, to whom be glory forever. Amen. (Rom. 11:33–36)

This is a most fitting text to use for the start of a worship service. In what way could we respond to the revelation of almighty God but to "kneel before the LORD our Maker" (Ps. 95:6)?
James K. A. Smith is helpful:

> In contrast to a worship service that vaguely begins when the music starts playing and parishioners slowly saunter in to join the crowd, a worship service that begins with the Call to Worship has already received a word from God who is active in worship and who *wants* us there. (Notice how, already, this framing of Christian worship is countercultural, displacing the priority of self and our desire to have the world available to us on *our* terms.) So the Call to Worship is a weekly reenactment of the primacy and sovereignty of the Creator in our lives.[4]

---

4. Smith, *You Are What You Love*, 96, emphasis original.

Invocation

The call must come with a response. Anytime God sends forth His word, He expects an answer (Isa. 55:11). The same is true in worship; it is a conversation, after all. So what is our response to this call to worship? What is our reply to this summons to do the most important thing there is? Easy: Help! That is, in essence, what the invocation is: a cry for help.

This, once again, is an extremely covenantal act. In the ancient covenants, the lesser king (the vassal) would call on the name of the greater king (the suzerain) in his time of crisis. It was the covenantal relationship that obligated the greater king to come to the rescue of the lesser. And in worship we call on the name of the almighty God in faith, trusting that He will come by His Spirit to enable the work He Himself has given us to do. Scripture records for us that ever since the fall, people have been calling "on the name of the LORD" (Gen. 4:26). That is what we are doing in the invocation; we call on (invoke) the name of the Lord. This is why so many Reformed liturgies over the years have used Psalm 124:8 as an invocation: "Our help is in the name of the LORD, who made heaven and earth." Another common invocation is Psalm 51:15: "O Lord, open my lips, and my mouth shall show forth Your praise." What is common to both is the idea that only God can be our help in worship; only God can enable us to give Him what He is asking of us.

God's Greeting

The great thing with Christian worship is that we begin with the gospel. So we have cried out for help, and immediately God responds with a word of peace to us, a blessing, a word that says, "Everything is going to be okay. By my grace, I'm going to help you." This is the part of the service known as the greeting, in which the minister raises his hands and blesses the people. He does this as God's representative, not as if he has power in and of himself to impart a divine blessing. Thus the words are not the minister's either, but they are God's. Generally, they are taken from the opening of one of the Epistles: "Grace, mercy, and peace from God our Father and Jesus Christ our Lord" (1 Tim. 1:2); or "Grace to you and peace from God the Father and our Lord Jesus Christ, who

gave Himself for our sins, that He might deliver us from this present
evil age, according to the will of our God and Father, to whom be glory
forever and ever. Amen" (Gal. 1:3–5).

At this point in the service, what is happening? We are acting out
God's truth as it comes to us in places like Joel 2:32:

> And it shall come to pass
> That whoever calls on the name of the LORD
> Shall be saved.

We have called on His name in the invocation, and now in the greeting we are reminded of the promise that God does not forsake those
who call on Him. He has saved us, and we can continue our worship
with expectation because He is equipping us for the task to which
He has called us. He does this by sending among us His Holy Spirit
(John 14:26).

All of this is so that God might keep covenant with us. Though we
are faithless covenant breakers, He mercifully draws us in to be renewed
and restored through worship. Michael Horton writes, "God will not
violate his oath but will descend in the power of his Spirit to take up
his throne among us and deliver us from the world, the flesh, and the
devil…so we call on him to be present among us by his Spirit, and we
listen as Zechariah's prophecy is fulfilled in our presence: 'They will call
on my name, and I will answer them. I will say, "This is my people"; and
each one will say, "The LORD is my God"'" (Zech. 13:9)."[5]

Does this not move us to praise?

---

5. Horton, *Better Way*, 149.

Discussion Questions

1. Why does worship rightly begin with a call from God's Word? What are the theological implications of this?

2. What is God calling us out of?

3. What is God calling us into?

4. What does the word *invocation* mean, and what does having one remind us of each week?

5. What is happening when God's greeting is pronounced by the minister?

Chapter 9

The Verdict Is Pronounced

Run, John, and work, the law commands,
yet finds me neither feet nor hands;
But sweeter news the gospel brings,
it bids me fly and lends me wings!
—John Berridge

Worship ought to kill us.

Are you awake now? Quite a startling thought, isn't it? And it's not mine—not the wording anyway. It comes from author, theologian, and educator Marva J. Dawn, who even lamented that this line, used as a chapter title in one of her books, was not provocative enough! What point was she trying to make with this kind of language? It's a very biblical one, in fact. The Christian life, paradoxically, begins with death. We must die to our sin so that we can live for Christ. And this is one of the works that the Holy Spirit performs in us when we, by faith, participate in worship. Dawn writes, "God's Word, rightly read and heard, will shake us up. It will kill us, for God cannot bear our sin and wants to put to death our self-centeredness.... Once worship kills us, we are born anew to worship God rightly."[1]

In this chapter, we want to focus on the *cleansing* aspect of our worship service, which is perhaps the most neglected part of the service in most churches today. This is a sad reality, especially when we examine covenantal worship after the fall—it was meaningless unless an atoning offering for sin was made. Yet many Protestant churches

---

1. Dawn, *Reaching Out without Dumbing Down*, 206.

have abandoned this portion of the service, which is generally made up
of three main components: the reading of God's law, the confession of
sin, and the declaration of God's pardon. Here we will learn that *God,
week in and week out, puts to death the old self of sin through the law and
brings to life and sustains a new creation in Christ through the proclamation of the gospel.*

What Happened?

Why do churches neglect the regular use of these elements of worship?
I have heard a variety of reasons. A common one is that the idea of
confession is too "Roman Catholic," and thus it is omitted from the
service in an attempt to be truly Reformed and Protestant. But confessing our sins directly to God is much different from confessing our sins
indirectly through the mediation of a priest, as in the Roman Catholic
practice known as confession. We firmly believe that the minister has
no power in and of himself to pronounce any kind of absolution on the
confessor. The minister stands as a representative of God—in the place
of God but not in place of God—to make a declaration that assures
the confessors what Scripture teaches: that if we confess our sins God
is faithful and just to cleanse us from all unrighteousness (1 John 1:9;
cf. 1 Tim. 2:5).

Another common objection—perhaps the most common
objection—is that reading God's law and confessing sins is awkward and
can potentially make visitors and guests feel uncomfortable. I wouldn't
disagree with that. It probably makes members and regular attendees
feel a bit uncomfortable too. It's supposed to! We're talking about sin,
after all. This reveals a major issue in the culture of the church: we have
capitulated to the felt needs rather than the real needs of the world.
What does the world "feel" that they need? To be comfortable, to be
anonymous, above all to be entertained. Decades ago the megachurch
movement tapped into this, and church attendance exploded. The
equation was simple: subtract anything that makes people feel uncomfortable and you will gain huge crowds.

But worship is not meant to be about our felt needs or our comfort.
As we have seen, it is about what God commands us to do. God commands that we meditate on His law and confess to Him our sins where

we have fallen short (Rom. 3:23). This should by no means be something we are ashamed to include in our liturgies. Rather, this is one of the high points of the service. Why? Because once we confess our sins, we have the joy of hearing God's declaration of pardon. From the words of Scripture on the lips of the minister, we are assured that in Christ we have a full and free remission of all our sin and guilt. We hear the law, we confess our failure, but then we hear the gospel.

Reading of the Law

It begins with reading God's law. Why should we read and hear God's law in a worship service? Is it to commemorate some aspect of our religious history? In the seminary I attended, every year our student body was reminded of the Consolidated Appropriations Acts, which required any institution that received federal funding to hold an educational program on the US Constitution on September 17. September 17 is officially Constitution Day, commemorating the day in 1787 when the signers at the Constitutional Convention in Philadelphia officially made it the law of the land. Since certain students received federal loans, on that day our attention was drawn to the text of the US Constitution.

Is that what we're doing when we read the law of God in church? Is every Sunday something of a "Constitution Day," when we commemorate the adoption of the law of the land? Is it mere historical observance? No—far from it! For one thing, unlike any human legal code, the law of the Lord is perfect, sure, right, pure, clean, true, righteous, more valuable than gold, and even sweeter than honey (Ps. 19:7–10). But beyond that, we read God's law precisely because it tells us how to live. For this reason, we see why the reading of the law comes early in the covenantal conversation of worship. As we saw with Israel at Sinai, once God calls His people together He says, "Now, since you're mine, this is how you're supposed to behave." It's God's rulebook for life. It's a big rulebook too. The law is not merely the Ten Commandments, although that is a comprehensive summary of it (even more succinct is Jesus's summary for us to love God and neighbor). The law is really anything and everything in Scripture that commands.

Anytime we find an imperative in the Bible, that's the law. It doesn't matter if it's "You shall not murder" (Ex. 20:13), or "Be hospitable to one another without grumbling" (1 Peter 4:9). It's God's will for us, and He has given it to us so that we don't need to wonder what our lives should look like in order to belong to Him. The Westminster divines put it this way: "[The law] is of great use to [believers], as well as to others; in that, as a rule of life informing them of the will of God, and their duty, it directs and binds them to walk accordingly" (WCF 19.6). God is a holy God, utterly separate from sin and any profane thing. And He has called us, as His children, to be holy just as He is holy (1 Peter 1:16). The law tells us how to do that.

But the law tells us something else: it tells us that we *haven't* done that. It tells us that we *can't* do that! The law discovers and uncovers the "sinful pollutions" of our "nature, heart, and lives" (WCF 19.6). As we sit under God's law, we hear all the ways we have failed our Lord in thought, word, and deed by what we have done and even by what we have left undone (in the words of an old prayer). So we read God's law to be put in our place. It's an act of submitting to God as Lord over our lives. We don't get to call the shots; He does—and has—in His holy law.

The trend in modern evangelical worship services to exclude reading or reflection on God's holy law is completely foreign to biblical worship. Consider that within the holy place of the tabernacle, the meeting place of God, was the ark of the covenant. The ark symbolized God's presence, and within the ark was a copy of the written law of God (Deut. 31:24–26). The law laid out the terms for the covenant relationship that God entered into with Israel, and these terms "were central to Israel's worship and never apart from it."[2] Old covenant worshipers could cry out, "Oh, how I love Your law!" (Ps. 119:97) because they knew that the law laid the foundation for their relationship with God. Therefore, the law is a necessary part of worship—a necessary part of meeting with God—as it tells us who He is and also who we are.

---

2. Bruce K. Waltke, *An Old Testament Biblical Theology* (Grand Rapids: Zondervan, 2007), 459.

Confession of Sin

The Duty of Confession

When we see that we are so often rebellious and disobedient, we are moved naturally from hearing God's law to confessing our sins. We are given a clear example of this progression in Nehemiah 8. The Israelites had returned from exile to reestablish the city of Jerusalem and the temple for worship. The great scribe Ezra came out and read aloud the law of God for the first time in a very long time and this is what happened:

> And Ezra opened the book [of the law of Moses] in the sight of all the people....
>
> Then all the people answered, "Amen, Amen!" while lifting up their hands. And they bowed their heads and worshiped the LORD with their faces to the ground....
>
> The Levites...helped the people to understand the Law; and the people stood in their place. So they read distinctly from the book, in the Law of God; and they gave the sense, and helped them to understand the reading....
>
> [And] all the people wept, when they heard the words of the Law. (Neh. 8:5–9)

As the law was read, the people were humbled. They fell on their faces in a sign of contrition. They were moved to tears of sorrow over their sin. A similar thing happened at an earlier point in Israel's history when King Josiah discovered the law after it had been neglected for years (2 Kings 22:11). This very important liturgical pattern is also seen in Isaiah 6, when Isaiah was brought before God's presence, and before His beauty and majesty, he was forced to conclude,

> Woe is me, for I am undone!
> Because I am a man of unclean lips,
> And I dwell in the midst of a people of unclean lips;
> For my eyes have seen the King,
> The LORD of hosts. (v. 5)

Confession naturally and logically follows after being exposed to God's holiness, especially as it is revealed in His law.

I have already noted that people don't like the idea of confession. But God does, and it's His will for us that when we hear His law we examine our lives against it and that we subsequently confess our sins where we have fallen short. We have biblical precedent for this—not just privately but even in a public and corporate setting of worship. Nehemiah 9 is one long chapter of confession in a corporate worship service. Psalms 32 and 51, though penned as personal confessions, would go on to be used by all Israel in the temple. First John 1:8 puts it bluntly for us: "If we say that we have no sin, we deceive ourselves, and the truth is not in us." John is saying churches that abandon confession in their worship are feeding into a delusion. We are sinners, and sinners need to confess.

"But," some people might object, "why should I have to confess my sins if I have already done it once and therefore have been freely forgiven and accepted by Jesus Christ?" The reality is that even though we are saved, sin still lives in us. We've been taken out of the world of sin (Col. 1:13), but sin hasn't completely been taken out of us (Rom. 6:1–2, 12). So as we come to God in confession, particularly in corporate worship, we are reminding ourselves of our identity: we are those who have been forgiven, but we are not perfect. We are, in the words of Martin Luther, "*simul justus et peccator*": simultaneously justified and sinful. This is what we experience this side of heaven. To neglect confession is to risk thinking we are sinless saints who have no need of God after all. So yes, even if we are already Christians, we continue to be confessors as well. "We are always becoming Christians 'again' every day.... Repentance and faith are always renewed daily."[3] Confession of and sorrow over and turning from sin must all be part of the regular makeup of our lives. Let them therefore be part of the regular makeup of our worship as well.

The Beauty of Confession
We have been speaking of the duty of confession, but we should not neglect the inherent beauty of it as well. We know from Paul's letter to the Romans that even if we deny the existence of God, our consciences still nag at us and tell us He's there and we aren't on good terms (2:15).

---

3. Horton, *Better Way*, 150.

Everyone knows they need to confess, but perhaps they just don't know how. So rather than shamefully dismissing this portion from our worship services on account of seeker sensitivity, shouldn't we see this as a wonderful opportunity for people to do the very thing they know they need to do? Whether they can articulate it or not, people want to confess. There is both a spiritual and a physical catharsis that comes from confession—it's a freeing exercise. To withhold confession in worship is to keep people in bondage. Far from being awkward, confession is where true peace is found.

David recognized this in Psalm 32. To abstain from confession was tantamount to a slow, painful death:

> When I kept silent, my bones grew old
> Through my groaning all the day long.
> For day and night Your hand was heavy upon me;
> My vitality was turned into the drought of summer. (vv. 3–4)

In terms of our sin, silence will mean suffering. But the moment we open our hearts and our mouths and confess our guilt, we receive healing, as David experienced:

> I acknowledged my sin to You,
> And my iniquity I have not hidden;
> I said, "I will confess my transgressions to the LORD,"
> And You forgave the iniquity of my sin. (v. 5)

One of the greatest gifts of worship is the curative power of confession.

Throughout the church's history, this has manifested itself in various ways in the worship service. For example, while serving as a pastor in Strasbourg, John Calvin structured his liturgy to include a confession of sin immediately following the call to worship. Thomas Cranmer placed confession immediately before the distribution of the elements of the Lord's Supper. In the Directory for the Publick Worship of God, the Westminster divines did not include a separate prayer of confession but rather suggested that it be included along with other petitions in the "great prayer" (what we might today call the congregational or pastoral prayer) leading up to the sermon.

There are numerous ways to approach this important aspect of worship; the critical thing is that confession is present. As worship inevitably shapes and forms the way we think about God, ourselves, and the world around us, we desperately need this repeated confrontation with the holiness of God and our own sinfulness. It lays the foundational understanding without which no one can be saved.

The earliest liturgical window we have into the post-apostolic church is in a first-century document known as the Didache, Greek for "teaching." The Didache lays forth several principles and practices for worship services. Its comments on confession are brief but profound and aptly summarize the importance of this discipline: "Confess your sins in church, and do not go to prayer with a guilty conscience. This is the Way of Life."

Declaration of Pardon

When we confess we are indeed freed because immediately after, we hear God's declaration of forgiveness in Jesus Christ. Whereas John tells us we are self-deluded if we don't confess, he also tells us that if we do, God "is faithful and just to forgive us our sins and to cleanse us from all unrighteousness" (1 John 1:9). The declaration of pardon, also sometimes called the assurance of pardon or the absolution or, even more archaically, "the comfortable words," is the part of the service in which the minister declares to the congregation that if they are in Christ, they have forgiveness of sins. Far from the Roman Catholic notion, the minister cannot impart any kind of divine forgiveness on anyone. All he can do is assure the people of what God's Word says. He makes this declaration in his role as the mouthpiece of God.

Once again, we need to guard ourselves from thinking that reading the law, confessing our sins, and hearing about our forgiveness are just mundane, rote exercises on any given Sunday. Worship is not just when we are singing. It's not just when we hear someone preach. It's from the call to worship to the benediction. And so we need to be cognizant of what is happening in this cleansing portion of the service. God has given us His law, revealed to us how horribly we have broken it, and then in grace declares that we have nothing to fear even though we are awful sinners. It's astounding. It doesn't make any sense—but that's grace for you! "There is therefore now no condemnation to those who are in Christ Jesus" (Rom. 8:1).

I have said that corporate worship is the tangible, livable story of the gospel retold week by week. In each portion of the service we flesh out more of who we are and what part we play in that story. The reading of the law and confession of sin remind us that we are sinners. Wouldn't it be awful if it all ended there? Yet as believers we discover in the declaration of pardon that we are not just sinners, but we are sinners saved by grace. We are those who are cleansed, forgiven, and pardoned in Christ. Up to this point there is conflict and suspense in the story. It doesn't appear that we will make it out of this encounter with a holy God! Our fate seems sealed in judgment and destruction. There's a tension. But then the sweet resolution comes when we hear of our rescue. We are right with God—but not in and of ourselves. We are right with God because of Jesus. That's who we are in the story: the people who have been rescued by Christ. That identity must be stamped on us again and again so that we will believe it, and in believing it be conformed to it!

So what is happening when we worship? We stand before almighty God, the Judge, the one who gets the final say. We stand before Him and hear His laws read, and we recognize that we have broken them all. We are cosmic convicts. We stand condemned before this law. But then God pronounces the verdict: *not guilty*! We come to be joyfully assured of Christ's once-for-all sacrifice, which atones for all our sin and all our guilt. In the old covenant, the cleansing cycle of worship meant people had to actually enact ritual cleanliness, and this included a lot of blood. For us in our new covenant worship, we hear about blood, but we don't spill any. We hear about Jesus's blood, which has freed us from our sins (Rev. 1:5), ransomed us from bondage (1 Peter 1:18–19), cleansed us from unrighteousness (1 John 1:7–9), and brought us near to God (Eph. 2:13).

What could be better than that?

Law and Gospel

Perhaps the most important theological distinction every Christian must master is that of law and gospel. All Scripture can be divided under these two headings: passages that command (law), or passages that promise (gospel). Theodore Beza, who succeeded John Calvin at Geneva, wrote in *The Christian Faith* (1558), "Ignorance of this distinction between Law and Gospel is one of the principal sources of the abuses which corrupted and still corrupt Christianity."[4] The ignorance that Beza wrote of could lead to abuses like legalism (thinking you are saved by good works) at one end of the spectrum, or antinomianism (thinking that good works don't matter at all) at the other end. Ultimately, the greatest tragedy for those who mix up this distinction would be missing out on heaven because salvation is not something that we can earn. It doesn't come about through obedience to command; it comes about through faithful reception of God's promise. So while the distinction may seem simple, it has profound implications for life in the here-and-now, as well as for your eternal life in the hereafter.

Thus we find another reason why this portion of the liturgy is so crucial: it lays out the proper distinction between the law and the gospel, putting each in their appropriate place. First, we learn from God's law what is required in order to be saved. We learn of God's strict standard for eternal communion with Him, and we also learn that we cannot meet that standard. But then comes the glorious good news. We are kept from thinking that the law is the means of salvation. We instead learn that "what the law could not do in that it was weak through the flesh, God did by sending His own Son in the likeness of sinful flesh, on account of sin" (Rom. 8:3). What the law cannot do, the gospel does. We hear that God has paved a way for us to know Him through the gracious merits of His Son. This portion of the worship service sets forth in a powerful, almost palpable way the distinction between law and gospel.

And it must be said that believing the gospel then utterly transforms the way we relate to the law. Having been pardoned, I no longer see the law as something that only condemns me, but I see it as my guide for living a life of gratitude to God. I now want to completely obey the law not to earn my righteousness before God but because He has given me a righteousness through Jesus Christ. Now I make it my aim to please Him (2 Cor. 5:9). This is why in some liturgies the order

---

4. As quoted in R. Scott Clark, "Is the Law/Gospel Distinction Only Lutheran?," *The Heidelblog: Recovering the Reformed Confession* (blog), October 18, 2008, https://heidelblog.net/2008/10/is-the-lawgospel-distinction-only-lutheran/.

is slightly reversed: recognizing they come before a holy God, the congregation begins with confession, hears the gospel in the declaration of pardon, and only then comes the reading of the Decalogue.[5] The law then functions as a call to grateful and humble obedience to those who know their redeemed status in Christ. This is essentially the pattern followed in many of the New Testament Epistles: the legal imperatives (what we must do) rarely come until after the announcement of the gospel indicatives (what God has done for us in Christ).[6]

Two Ways

I find the opening questions of catechisms to be fascinating, as they often frame what the authors deemed to be of greatest theological and practical importance. The Heidelberg Catechism is therefore one that is couched in the comfort of belonging to Jesus Christ as Savior and Master ("What is your only comfort in life and in death?"). The Westminster Shorter Catechism seeks to unpack how we can know and fulfill our purpose in life ("What is the chief end of man?"). A lesser-known catechism was written by William Twisse in 1645 and was titled *A Brief Catechetical Exposition of Christian Doctrine*. Twisse was an English Puritan and the first moderator of the Westminster Assembly. His catechism is made up of several lessons, with each lesson containing a series of questions and answers. Consider the way Twisse opens up his catechism:

> Q. How many ways does the Word of God teach us to come to the Kingdom of Heaven?
> A. Two.
>
> Q. What are those two ways?
> A. By the Law and the Gospel.

---

5. This is one of the ways John Calvin structured his worship service in Strasbourg. See Gibson and Earngey, *Reformation Worship*, 305.

6. For example, see Ephesians 4:25–6:20. This passage, loaded with imperatives, comes only after Paul has established that the "old man" (4:20–24) has been put to death and we are now defined by the new life in Jesus Christ.

Q. What does the Law teach us?
A. "Do this and you shall live."

Q. What does the Gospel teach us?
A. "Believe in the Lord Jesus and you shall be saved."

Q. Can we come to the Kingdom of Heaven by the way of God's Law?
A. No.

Q. Why not?
A. Because we cannot keep the Law.

Q. Why can't we keep the Law?
A. Because we are all born in sin....

Q. Which way then do you hope to enter to the Kingdom of Heaven?
A. By the Gospel.

Q. What is the Gospel?
A. The glad tidings of salvation by Jesus Christ....

This is the first lesson: to know the right way to the Kingdom of Heaven, and this consists in knowing the difference between the Law and the Gospel.[7]

Worship is meant to train us for kingdom living, as well as open up the doors of the kingdom for those who are unsaved. Since knowing the right way to the kingdom consists in a proper knowledge of the law and the gospel, and especially how they relate to one another, they must each play a prominent place in our gathered worship.

---

7. William Twisse, *A Brief Catechetical Exposition of Christian Doctrine*, ed. C. Matthew McMahon, http://reformedfaithmission.weebly.com/uploads/8/3/0/9/8309462/brief-catechetical-exposition-of-christian-doctrine-cathechisms-william-twisse.pdf.

Discussion Questions

1. Why do you think many churches no longer read God's law?

2. What work does the Spirit accomplish through the reading of God's law?

3. Why does confession of sin matter in worship?

4. What is happening when we receive a declaration of pardon?

5. Explain the law/gospel distinction. Why is this so essential?

Chapter 10

Jesus Gets Up to Preach

The preaching of the Word of God is the Word of God.
—Second Helvetic Confession (1562)

Many churches are abandoning thoughtful, Bible-based sermons because they feel they don't speak to the culture. So what does? TED talks. Though the organization has been around for decades, TED (technology, education, and design) talks began in earnest a little over ten years ago and have now skyrocketed in popularity. You've likely seen some of these presentations, or clips of some: a recognized authority on a subject stands on an empty stage, the auditorium is darkly lit, perhaps there is a screen behind the speaker (there is certainly the iconic red-lighted TED logo somewhere on stage). The expert walks around casually and shares fascinating insights about his or her respective field to an enraptured audience.

People have analyzed these talks. What makes them so popular and engaging? The presentation is sleek, for one. Slides are often used, but not of the standard PowerPoint quality. There is not an overabundance of charts, bullet points, or texts, nor are there overly adventurous transitions. The graphics are professionally done, and the information on the screen is almost always conveyed through images, not text. The time limit is another factor. No TED talk is permitted to be longer than eighteen minutes. This not only helps hook an audience of rising millennials and Generation Zs, with their notoriously short attention spans, but "it's also the perfect length if you want your message to go viral."[1]

It's no wonder solid, in-depth preaching is falling by the wayside if the goal is now sleek presentation and viral potential. Maybe we need to take a cue from the scientists and sociologists who have determined the perfect presentation model for our twenty-first-century audience. Maybe we need shorter sermons and more pictures. Or maybe not. Maybe there's another way. My conviction is that if we knew what was actually happening in truly biblical, Spirit-wrought preaching, we would feel much differently about sermons. We would approach preaching in an entirely different manner. So what is happening in the sermon? Let me suggest this answer: *by the power of the Holy Spirit, Jesus speaks through His ordained servant, saving sinners by the spoken word to the glory of God.*

Think about that for a minute. I am saying that in true preaching, Jesus Christ Himself is the one who is actually speaking. If that's true, can you imagine cutting the sermon short by fifteen or twenty minutes, or demanding an eighteen-minute cap? Can you imagine pulling out your smartphone and scrolling through social media to help the time go by? Can you imagine doing anything besides giving your full and undivided attention to the King of kings and the Lord of lords, who has come into your presence and is speaking directly to you? It might sound too miraculous, but this is truly what is going on during this portion of the worship service. Thus, it is the preached word that consecrates, or sets apart, a people for God Himself. It is the preaching of God's word—through the power of the Holy Spirit—that calls people out of their sin into salvation in Jesus Christ alone.

The Witness of the Apostolic Church

As we look at the biblical data, we see that this definition of preaching is not all that radical. The church believed that when the apostles preached, the voice of Christ could be heard. How else can we make

---

1. Anne Fisher, "Why TED Talks Are Better than the Last Speech You Sat Through," *Fortune*, February 25, 2014, https://fortune.com/2014/02/25/why-ted-talks-are-better-than-the-last-speech-you-sat-through/.

sense of Paul's claim in Ephesians 2:17 that Christ "came and preached…
to you" when there was no Christian church at Ephesus during the
life of Christ, and certainly therefore He did not preach there during
His earthly ministry? The way we make sense of this is the same way
the apostles did: when they preached the word, Christ was speaking
through them. Similarly, Romans 10:14 equates the voice of preachers
with the voice of Jesus: "How shall they believe in Him of whom they
have not heard?" is legitimately translated "in Him *whom* they have not
heard?" This teaching has been famously codified in the opening chapter of the Second Helvetic Confession (1562), in which the Reformer
Heinrich Bullinger powerfully wrote, "The preaching of the Word of
God is the Word of God."

It might sound arrogant or audacious to claim that God Himself is
speaking through the pastor each week. After all, this is just a normal
guy. You know him. He drives a normal car, he doesn't have the greatest
style, and through babysitting experience you may know that he has
unruly kids. Nothing seems divine about him—and indeed, nothing is.
God doesn't transform the preacher; God uses the preacher. Far from
being a braggadocious claim on the role of the minister, this understanding humbles humanity and glorifies God. Paul speaks of this in
1 Corinthians 2:3–5: "I was with you in weakness, in fear, and in much
trembling. And my speech and my preaching were not with persua-
sive words of human wisdom, but in demonstration of the Spirit and
of power, that your faith should not be in the wisdom of men but in
the power of God." Many men in ministry today might be surprised
to learn that the most successful missionary and church planter who
ever lived did not rely on innovations or seeker-sensitive appeals—only
God's word! Indeed, his ministry advice to his apprentice Timothy was
to "give attention to" (coming from that same Greek root word in Acts
2:42, "persevere in") the public reading of Scripture (1 Tim. 4:13) and to
"preach the word!" (2 Tim. 4:2).

Perhaps we have no clearer teaching on this matter than in 1 Peter
4:11. There Peter says we need to recognize that those who get up to
preach are really instruments of God—channels by which Christ Himself speaks to His people: "If anyone speaks [that is, preaches], let him
speak as the oracles of God." When we recognize it's God's word—and

not man's—that should be coming from the preacher's lips, then we can start to make sense of how something as simple and foolish as preaching can have such marvelous results! Thus the Westminster Shorter Catechism 89 says, "The Spirit of God maketh the reading, but especially the preaching, of the word, an effectual means of convincing and converting sinners, and of building them up in holiness and comfort, through faith, unto salvation."

This is precisely why when we examine the apostolic church, we find that church growth is invariably attributed to the preaching of the word. In Acts we read the following:

> And they continued steadfastly in the apostles' doctrine.... And the Lord added to the church daily those who were being saved. (2:42, 47)

> Many of those who heard the word believed; and the number of the men came to be about five thousand. (4:4)

> Then the word of God spread, and the number of the disciples multiplied greatly in Jerusalem, and a great many of the priests were obedient to the faith. (6:7)

> While Peter was still speaking these words, the Holy Spirit fell upon all those who heard the word. (10:44)

> The word of God grew and multiplied. (12:24)

> Now when the Gentiles heard this, they were glad and glorified the word of the Lord. And as many as had been appointed to eternal life believed.
>
> And the word of the Lord was being spread throughout all the region. (13:48–49)

The evidence is quite overwhelming. In all these instances we see that the *church grows* because the *word goes*. This word is not the mere teaching of man but the "word of God," and it increases because the Holy Spirit moves in the hearts of those who hear it to receive it. This is why the church continued steadfastly in the apostles' preaching. The term used in Acts 2:42 means "to persevere in"—in other words, they didn't give up on preaching. Maybe some weeks the sermon was less interesting than others. Maybe some weeks more people were converted than others. It didn't matter what emotions they felt or what results they could see—no matter what, they were devoted to, committed to, and fixated on the preaching of God's word. And why? Because they understood it was the means by which their Savior, King, and Head communicated Himself to them. They devoted themselves to the apostles' preaching because they knew that when they did, they were really devoting themselves to Christ.

The Foolishness of Preaching

We are given a hint as to why it's the preaching that the Spirit blesses: so "that [our] faith should not be in the wisdom of men but in the power of God" (1 Cor. 2:5). Paul is even more explicit in the verses leading up to this one, giving us a look into his own theology of preaching:

> For Christ did not send me to baptize, but to preach the gospel, not with wisdom of words, lest the cross of Christ should be made of no effect.
>
> For the message of the cross is foolishness to those who are perishing, but to us who are being saved it is the power of God....
>
> For since, in the wisdom of God, the world through wisdom did not know God, it pleased God through the foolishness of the message preached to save those who believe. (1:17–18, 21)

Let's take a moment to unpack what we find in these verses to better understand what exactly goes on in worship when preaching takes place.

A Sending Christ

The first thing Paul says is that he preaches because he has been commissioned to do so by Jesus Christ Himself. "Christ did not send me to baptize, but to preach the gospel" (1 Cor. 1:17). Being sent by Christ is prerequisite of what it means to be an apostle. *Apostle* comes from the verb *apostellō*, which means "to send a message"—so an apostle is literally one who is sent to speak. In New Testament terms more specifically, an apostle is one who is sent by Christ to speak on His behalf.

Jesus says as much to His disciples in John 20:21: "As the Father has sent Me, I also send you." So it should come as no surprise to us that Paul says he has been sent by Christ to preach.

But there is something we can learn here that is true of all preachers, not just the apostles: they are sent by Christ. While preachers today are not sent personally by Jesus Christ as the apostles were, the New Testament understanding is that all preachers at any time will be sent in the name of Christ—that is, to represent Him. Julius Kim explains that "one of the primary images used to convey the identity of a preacher [in the New Testament] is the *herald*.... The herald became the voice of the king. Though the words that he spoke came from his own mouth, the words represented another, more powerful one, whose words had authority."[2]

This is how we must view preaching today. A preacher is one who represents another. He is heralding a message from the great King, Christ Jesus. It's the Lord's message we are hearing, and no one else's. The message belongs so intimately to Christ that it is as though He were the one in the pulpit. One of my favorite comments on preaching comes from J. I. Packer's reflection on the ministry of Martyn Lloyd-Jones. According to Packer, the effectiveness of Lloyd-Jones's ministry was his ability to let Christ speak in the sermon. In his preaching it was as if Lloyd-Jones "slips out of the picture and leaves us with the God whom he would have us know."[3] True preaching doesn't present the preacher; it presents the sending Christ.

A Simple Message

Looking again at 1 Corinthians 1:17, notice that Paul makes a point to say that Christ has sent him to preach a very simple message. He doesn't come to preach "with the wisdom of words," or cleverness of speech. Why does Paul make this comment? In that Hellenistic Greek culture there was a preoccupation with gifted storytellers and rhetoricians who could capture an audience's attention. Put more bluntly, though, Paul

---

2. Julius J. Kim, *Preaching the Whole Counsel of God* (Grand Rapids: Zondervan, 2015), 19, emphasis original.

3. As quoted in Iain H. Murray, *David Martyn Lloyd-Jones: The Fight of Faith 1939–1981* (Edinburgh: Banner of Truth, 1990), 325–26.

says this because he knows "people often like the preacher more than his message."[4]

If preaching were about the preacher's skill, abilities, and charm, the cross would be emptied of its power. It's not that the cross would suddenly become powerless, but rather that people would not be seeing the power of the cross at all! Or put another way, the herald would be obscuring the view of the King who sent him. When preaching becomes about entertaining jokes, quaint illustrations, feel-good stories, or self-help tips, Christ is no longer seen. And He is no longer seen because He certainly is not sending that kind of preacher. It is a simple message that ensures we see and know the sending Christ. And what is the content of this simple message? "Christ and Him crucified" (1 Cor. 2:2).

A Saving Power

Even though the message is simple, it's because it reveals the life-giving Christ that Paul can say with confidence that preaching has a saving power: "For the message of the cross is foolishness to those who are perishing, but to us who are being saved [the message of the cross] is the power of God" (1 Cor. 1:18). Calvin paraphrases this verse as follows: "The preaching of the cross, as having nothing of human wisdom to recommend it to esteem, is reckoned foolishness by them that perish; in our view, notwithstanding, the wisdom of God clearly shines forth in it."[5] While to unbelievers it seems like utter nonsense, to those who recognize it as God's wisdom, it is the means of salvation (cf. Rom. 1:16). In the words of Puritan Matthew Poole, preaching is "the sacred means by which [God] would bring all those that give credit to the revelation of it, and receive Christ held forth in it, to eternal life and salvation."[6]

If it is not already clear by this point, it is worth noting that God loves preaching. He loves it because He loves saving sinners, and this is how He saves them. We can despise preaching all we want. We can replace preaching with productions, play movies instead of opening up the Bible, or do whatever we think is going to win people—and indeed

---

4. Kim Riddlebarger, *First Corinthians* (Powder Springs, Ga.: Tolle Lege, 2013), 21.

5. John Calvin, *Calvin's Commentaries* (Grand Rapids: Baker, 1981), 20:78.

6. Matthew Poole, *Matthew Poole's Commentary on the Holy Bible* (Edinburgh: Banner of Truth, 1979), 3:542.

it might bring in more numbers, but it won't win more souls. So we too should love preaching. We should love it when our pastor steps into the pulpit to deliver God's word because it's a moment of salvation for God's chosen people. We should be pleased with preaching because it pleases God. Indeed, "it pleased God by the foolishness of preaching to save them that believe" (1 Cor. 1:21 KJV).

It's a mystery, but in God's wise plan, He has made it so that through simple words His saving work is made known.

The Wisdom of Man

The "wisdom" of men rejects this. Yet since the beginning of the world, God has been showing just what immense power is contained in His word, and He is doing the same in preaching today. John Calvin says that "no real union or perfection is attained, but by the outward preaching.... Those who neglect or despise this order choose to be wiser than Christ."[7]

Sadly, many churches do "despise" preaching, or at least in the way in which the apostles would have understood it. Instead of resting on the wisdom of God, many churches turn to human wisdom. The mystical aesthetic deems that preaching is too intellectual, so sermons are cut for time and watered down theologically. The entertainment aesthetic, much more prevalent in our current context, says that preaching is too boring. This wisdom has produced tricks, trends, and techniques in worship, gospel-centered sermons giving way to gimmick-centered services. The lights go down, the screen flashes some sleek graphics—it all begins to look a bit like a TED talk. Preaching becomes performing. Exhortation becomes presentation. It is all in an attempt to grow the church, of course. Yet as we've seen already, the scriptural data says that church growth is the result of the true preaching of the word.

Many are convinced this is too simple, too plain. Surely preaching can't have that kind of power. To many people in mainstream evangelicalism, the expositional preaching of God's word as a means of growth and expansion is utter foolishness. And sadly, it must be said, when a "church" deems this to be the case, they reveal themselves to be more

---

7. As quoted in Payne, *In the Splendor of Holiness*, 86.

a part of the world than actually a part of Christ's body. Michael Horton assesses the situation by writing that "surrounded by gimmicks and slick marketing, we assume that evangelism, church growth, and worship are subject to the same rules of persuasion as anything else. If we believe that salvation is essentially in our hands, it follows that it is up to us to determine the most effective strategy for reaching the lost."[8]

Salvation, of course, is not in our hands. If the church truly believes that, if the church recognizes that salvation belongs to Christ, then it ought to proclaim Christ, preach Christ, and promote Christ. That is the apostolic pattern laid out for us in Scripture—"Him we preach" (Col. 1:28). But as it stands, the gimmicks employed to bring in crowds on Sunday are the same ones employed to keep them there week after week. That is why in such churches we hear much more about the music, the coffee, the convenience, or the experience long before we hear about the importance of the preached word in a worship service. The oft-quoted aphorism is right: "What you win them with, you win them to."

That is why we must never stray from the simple means of grace: word, sacrament, and prayer (WSC 88). There is a time to be savvy and wise about reaching out into communities to gain more visitors—I do not deny that—but never at the sake of neglecting the means of grace. After all, to use the language of the Westminster Confession, these means are what "gathers" in the saints (WCF 25.3). D. G. Hart states that "the Word inscripturated and the Word incarnate are specific about the right techniques for church growth: the divinely given and divinely commanded means of Word and sacrament."[9] Echoing this thought in his excellent article titled "The Ordinary Means of Growth," Ligon Duncan writes, "Nothing else we do in the church's program of ministry should detract from these central instruments of grace, and indeed everything else we do should promote and coalesce with them."[10]

---

8. Horton, *Better Way*, 61.
9. Hart, *Recovering Mother Kirk*, 47.
10. Ligon Duncan, "The Ordinary Means of Growth," *Tabletalk Magazine*, October 1, 2007, https://www.ligonier.org/learn/articles/ordinary-means-growth/.

The Power of God

What the church culture needs is a rediscovery of the power that is packed into a sermon. It's not a motivational speech; it's not a self-help seminar. *It's a supernatural moment where God raises dead people from the grave.* That's what is happening when the Scriptures are proclaimed and the gospel is preached. In the Westminster Assembly's Directory for the Publick Worship of God (1645) we find a statement that captures the essence of preaching: "Preaching of the word, being the power of God unto salvation, and one of the greatest and most excellent works belonging to the ministry of the gospel, should be so performed, that the workman need not be ashamed, but may save himself, and those that hear him."

What a grand assessment of preaching! According to the Westminster Assembly, preaching is "one of the greatest and most excellent" aspects of ministry. I don't think many Christians would echo that today. Based on the lack of solid, biblical preaching today, it would seem many churches don't either. And that must be because they are forgetting why preaching is so great and excellent: because it brings salvation.

We need to recover the zeal for God's word that the psalmist had when he declared: "Your testimonies are wonderful" (119:129). W. Robert Godfrey explains,

> What is being said there is not that God's testimonies inspire me to wonder, or that the testimonies are really, really great. They are not wonderful in that sense. Rather the Psalmist means that "Your testimonies are a miracle." The testimonies are a wonder that God has performed in the midst and in the sight of His people. In an age of fascination with signs and wonders, here is a great wonder. This is what the Scriptures teach. They are a wonder because God has inspired them, and God has inspired them not only to be true, but to be set specifically for the needs of His people.[11]

Do we recognize the wonder, or the miracle, that takes place when God's word is preached? The miracle is that the dead come to

---

11. W. Robert Godfrey, "The What and Why of Good Preaching," in *On Reforming Worship*, ed. David W. Hall and Jonathan L. Master (Powder Springs, Ga.: Covenant Foundation, 2018), 82.

life—and this indeed is our greatest need. And let this be a reminder for preachers to preach intentionally evangelistic sermons. That is, we are not merely to preach sermons anchored in God's word that reveal His nature, unfold biblical history, and explain theological truths. We must preach (and hear) sermons that also freely offer the gospel. If it's true that God uses preaching to save sinners, we should preach with an aim to do just that.

...Doomed to Repeat It

As the sermon recedes in importance today, we would do well to realize that we are repeating history. This was the state of things before the Reformation, when preaching was practically nonexistent. Unintelligible, unedifying services in Latin were commonplace. For both the clergy and the laity, the worship service was nothing other than a routine of mystical, merit-based rituals. The sermon had been tossed out the window because the Scriptures were seemingly so confounding. Hughes Oliphant Old writes, "[The Bible] more and more became a book of mysteries that could only be solved by mystical contemplation."[12] And elsewhere he states, "During the Dark Ages...Christian preaching receded in importance. More and more frequently public worship omitted even the simplest kind of sermon."[13]

The Reformers knew that strong expository preaching—that is, sermons based on Scripture—were essential to the worship of the early church. The condition of the Roman Church at that time was the exception, not the norm. Ulrich Zwingli, the Swiss Reformer, was the first significant figure to see that change was instituted in the church in regard to the preached word. The watershed moment came in January 1519, when he decided to preach in everyday German—rather than incomprehensible Latin—systematically through the Gospel of Matthew. This was seemingly unheard of in the last thousand years. Zwingli's decision to preach expository sermons week after week was well received by the masses: "Every man, woman, and child who could

---

12. Hughes Oliphant Old, *The Reading and Preaching of the Scriptures in the Worship of the Christian Church* (Grand Rapids: Eerdmans, 2002), 3:xvi.

13. Old, *Worship: Reformed according to Scripture*, 68.

possibly get there crammed into Zurich's Great Minster to hear him."[14] Sounds like the church growth we saw in Acts! Other Reformers soon followed suit: Luther, Calvin, and Bucer. As Terry Johnson says, "The Reformation was, if nothing else, a revolution in preaching."[15] Similarly, Hughes Oliphant Old comments that "with the sixteenth-century Reformation, biblical preaching once again took a prominent place in the regular worship of the church. People were eager to learn and eagerly sat under the pulpits of preachers who could expound to them the Holy Scriptures."[16]

The Reformers rightly believed that as they faithfully proclaimed God's word week in and week out, it was God speaking, not them. That's why preaching was so important back then and why it needs to be so important once again today. In preaching, the congregation hears God's very relevant word to them. Michael Horton explains this well and is worth quoting at some length:

> It is important for us to realize that preaching is effective not because of the minister or the people, the music, the staging and lighting, dramas, or other means that we might consider more effective than "the foolishness of preaching." It is effective because God has promised to dispense His saving grace then and there by His Spirit, and it grows organically out of the logic of the message itself because it is an announcement of something that has been accomplished by God, rather than an incentive to get sinners to save themselves by sheer force of will or effort. It is good news, not good advice, good production value, or good ideas.... Often God is not present where we would expect to find Him. But we can always count on God being where He has promised to meet us.... The power of the Spirit is linked to a promise; namely, a promise that faith comes by hearing the gospel preached.[17]

---

14. Old, *Worship: Reformed according to Scripture*, 71.
15. Johnson, *Worshipping with Calvin*, 104.
16. Old, *Worship: Reformed according to Scripture*, 70.
17. Horton, *Better Way*, 64–65.

Hearing Is Believing

I recently saw a trailer for a new miniseries dramatizing the life of the New Testament disciples, and in particular their interaction with Jesus. The tagline for the show caught my attention: "See Jesus as they did." The thought was that a historical, true-to-life reenactment of the first-century disciples that would give us a glimpse into the life of Christ was going to draw viewers. And it probably will. Don't you want to see Jesus, after all?

But the whole premise is unbiblical. While the message of our skeptic age is "seeing is believing," the message we find in Scripture is that *hearing* is believing. Don't get me wrong. We will see Jesus one day when He comes again (1 John 3:2), and that is our great hope and expectation. Until that time, however, God has appointed that "faith comes by hearing"—and hearing what? Nothing other than "the word of God" (Rom. 10:17)

We don't get to see Jesus, not yet. We do get to hear Him though. And when the Spirit applies that word so that we respond in faith, that's all we need to be saved. Yet we always want more, don't we? Actually, the disciples struggled with the same thing. After the resurrection, Thomas wanted to see the wounds. Do you remember the reply Jesus gives? "Have you believed because you have seen me? Blessed are those *who have not seen* and yet have believed" (John 20:29 ESV). We have every reason to content ourselves with hearing Jesus. By God's design, through Spirit-wrought faith, the ear, not the eye, is the channel of salvation.

This means we must strive to hear Jesus when we listen to the preacher speaking. We are not claiming that a preacher, de facto of his office, preaches "the very words of God" every time he enters the pulpit. But Scripture tells us that the same Holy Spirit who inspired the Scriptures of old illumines the preachers of today and those who hear them. It is when the Holy Spirit is at work that we will receive Christ Himself: "To them it was revealed that, not to themselves, but to us they were ministering the things which now have been reported to you *through those who have preached the gospel to you by the Holy Spirit sent from heaven*—things which angels desire to look into" (1 Peter 1:12).

Jesus's disciples said to Him that He alone has the words of life (John 6:68). We come to church because we expect to hear those very same words. If you don't, then you're wasting your time. True preachers preach because they expect that by the Holy Spirit the words of life will come from their lips. There is nothing any person can ever do to transfer any other person from the realm of darkness to the realm of light. Only God can do that. We need these words of life that come only from God—from Jesus Himself, for He is the Word of life. And this is why we determine to know nothing but Christ and Him crucified. This is why our rallying cry is "Him we preach!"

When Jesus preached in the New Testament, His sermons were focused on His being the fulfillment of all the Old Testament promises in bringing the kingdom of God. In other words, Jesus preached Himself, for He alone is the way, the truth, and the life. So since Jesus preached only Himself, it makes perfect sense that now as He preaches through His ordained servants, He continues to preach only Himself.

Remember, faith comes by hearing—and what kind of hearing? Hearing *the word of God*. It is only God's word to us that gives us faith and thereby consecrates us as no longer belonging to the world but to God. So come with eager anticipation to worship and in particular to attend to the preaching of God's word. It is through preaching that Christ sends His heralds to announce the good news. And through that preaching, by faith, you will be changed.

Discussion Questions

1. In what ways does preaching seem foolish to the world? How have churches sometimes tried to make up for this folly with their own innovations?

2. How is preaching the "power of God"?

3. What is a herald? What does this have to do with preaching and preachers?

4. How can it be said that we hear Christ through the preached word?

5. How does this challenge your understanding of the sermon in worship?

Chapter 11

God Feasts with Us

Oh, taste and see that the LORD *is good;*
Blessed is the man who trusts in Him!
—King David, Psalm 34:8

Ever since the beginning of time, worship has followed a pattern that culminates in a feast. In the sinless garden, the apex of worship was the gift to eat from the Tree of Life and live forever. In a remarkably parallel fashion, the redeemed cosmos will find its crowning joy around a table feasting at the marriage supper of the Lamb. Why the emphasis on eating?

It's not so much that God is a God of consumption as much as He is a God of communion. He delights to commune with His creatures, and a meal is one of the most powerful ways to experience and exercise communion with someone. We know this innately. After all, why do first dates often take place at restaurants? Why do we host and attend dinner parties? Why is it a sign of affection and service to cook someone a meal? God has made us to be a people who, quite literally, go with our gut. We naturally "crave the company and the delights of the table."[1] There is nothing more fundamentally or powerfully communal than a meal.[2] Feasting is a primary means of fellowship, and in worship we feast to fellowship with God. This feasting is rightly seen to be the

---

1. Earley, *Common Rule*, 49.

2. Tim Chester writes, "Meals slow things down... [forcing] you to be people oriented instead of task oriented. Sharing a meal is not the only way to build relationships, but it is number one on the list." *A Meal with Jesus: Discovering Grace, Community, and Mission around the Table* (Wheaton, Ill.: Crossway, 2011), 47.

pinnacle of worship, for what could be more wonderful than the almighty, all-powerful, holy God of the universe having pleasure to fellowship with us?

Although God held out the hope of us feasting with Him even before the fall, now living east of Eden we must recognize that the prospect of eating with God takes on an entirely new significance. Ever since sin entered the world, the only way we could ever hope to fellowship and commune with God is through the finished work of Christ. Communion is only possible this side of the cross. We come to the Table now through the "new and living way" that Christ has paved for us by His life, death, resurrection, and ascension (Heb. 10:20). Therefore, we rightly call this aspect of worship "the Lord's Supper"—that is, it is the Lord Jesus Christ who has made it possible. He is both the host and the meal itself. Truly, we cannot understand the sacrament of the Lord's Supper apart from the gospel.

And it really is all about the gospel. It is easy to think the sacraments (baptism and the Lord's Supper) are primarily things that we are doing for God. In this light, baptism becomes our dedication to serve the Lord, and the Lord's Supper becomes something of a frequent act of *re*dedication, recognizing we have failed Him and need to do better. While there is certainly an aspect of this to the sacraments—the Westminster Confession says that part of the Supper is the "further engagement in and to all duties which [believers] owe unto [Jesus]" (29.1)—first and foremost the sacraments are about what God has done and is doing for us.

So what exactly is the Lord's Supper displaying about the work of God in Christ for His church? What is the point of eating bread and drinking wine in church? Is it some bizarre ritual, or does it have real meaning and power? There is no quick answer since the Lord's Supper is as multifaceted as the gospel that it represents. But to help us capture just a small something of the supernatural wonder that takes place when we celebrate the Lord's Supper, I have found it helpful to consider it in the following way: *through the Lord's Supper, God's Spirit strengthens our faith, hope, and love in the finished work of Jesus Christ as believers really and truly feast on Him.*

As we explore these three aspects (faith, hope, love) of the Supper, the marvel of them all really does come back to the sheer fact that we are granted the gift of eating with God. As one theologian puts it, "The Supper is most profoundly an ordinance of communion with the Savior. Through faith, the believer meets with Christ who spiritually nourishes his or her soul in that meal."[3] Our response to this aspect of worship can only be more worship—more praise, more adoration, more thanksgiving! Or, in the words of another old hymn, we ought to

> Bless the One whose grace unbounded
> this amazing banquet founded;
> he, tho' heav'nly, high, and holy,
> deigns to dwell with you most lowly.[4]

A Feast of Faith

First, let's explore in what ways the Lord's Supper strengthens our faith in the finished work of Christ. This is perhaps what first comes to mind when we consider the purpose of the sacrament: it's a means to *look back in faith* to what Jesus has done for us on the cross. This is a proper starting place; after all, it is what Jesus Himself expressly laid out as a purpose of the Supper: "Do this in remembrance of Me" (Luke 22:19).

Covenant Confirmation

As worship takes place in the context of a covenantal relationship, it is helpful to see how remembrance was a crucial aspect of covenants. In the ancient world, the entire covenant hinged on the suzerain (the greater king) remembering his promise to the vassal (the weaker king), and the vassal remembering his obligation to the suzerain. If either of these parties forgot their part in the covenant, the bond would be severed. Often, certain signs or symbols would be exchanged as reminders of the promises or obligations of the covenant—and the same is true with God's covenants to humanity. Guy Waters writes, "When we look

3. Guy Prentiss Waters, *The Lord's Supper as the Sign and Meal of the New Covenant* (Wheaton, Ill.: Crossway, 2019), 93–94.

4. Johann Franck, "Soul, Adorn Yourself with Gladness" (1649), trans. Catherine Winkworth (1858), in *Trinity Hymnal*.

at the various covenants that God made with people in Scripture, a
striking pattern emerges—God appointed a sign to accompany the covenant that he made.… Each sign was given to the covenant community
as a visible and perpetual reminder of God's goodness in and through
that particular covenant."[5]

Consider the covenant with Noah. There we find God appropriates
the rainbow to be a sign of remembrance—not for humanity but for
Himself!

> I set My rainbow in the cloud, and it shall be for the sign of the
> covenant between Me and the earth. It shall be, when I bring a
> cloud over the earth, that the rainbow shall be seen in the cloud;
> and I will remember My covenant which is between Me and you
> and every living creature of all flesh; the waters shall never again
> become a flood to destroy all flesh. The rainbow shall be in the
> cloud, and I will look on it to remember the everlasting covenant
> between God and every living creature of all flesh that is on the
> earth. (Gen. 9:13–16)

Think also of the scene in which God proclaimed to Abraham the
covenant of grace: "Do not be afraid, Abram. I am your shield, your
exceedingly great reward" (Gen. 15:1). You would think that word of
promise from God Himself would be enough, but it wasn't. Abraham
still doubted, asking how God could possibly make something great out
of his miserable situation (vv. 2–3). What does God do? He does not
give Abraham a newer, better promise. Rather, God gives him a way of
confirming and remembering the original one:

> Then He brought him outside and said, "Look now toward
> heaven, and count the stars if you are able to number them." And
> He said to him, "So shall your descendants be."
>   And he believed in the LORD, and He accounted it to him for
> righteousness. (vv. 5–6)

The stars of the night sky were a confirmation to Abraham of God's
covenant of grace with him and his family. We could say they acted as

---

5. Waters, Lord's Supper, 45.

a sacrament in this instance. Every time Abraham stepped outside at night, he *remembered* what God had promised.

Memorial Meal

There are overt parallels to the old covenant Passover and our new covenant Lord's Supper. One of the major ways the new echoes the old is in this theme of remembrance. Moses tells Israel they are to observe the feast of Passover every year lest they forget what God had done for them: "Remember this day in which you went out of Egypt, out of the house of bondage; for by strength of hand the LORD brought you out of this place" (Ex. 13:3). Each year the people would have a meal to aid their memory, the roasted lamb acting as a visceral reminder of the blood required to spare and rescue them.

At the institution of the Lord's Supper, Jesus picked up this same theme but said that now all true believers are to remember something different, something newer, something better than the Passover. It is a greater rescue, a greater salvation—indeed, a greater Lamb. Jesus gives us bread and wine as a means of awakening our faith to the mighty work of salvation that He accomplished with His body and blood on the cross. That's what we're meant to think back on as we partake of this meal. That's what it means to "do this in remembrance of Me."

It is pretty remarkable the way in which our senses are linked to our memory. Certain sounds, tastes, or smells lodge themselves into our brain at a fixed time and place, so that whenever we encounter them again we are drawn back in our minds to that former situation. But this varies from person to person depending on our experiences. For example, when my wife and I get a whiff of the same musty smell we recall two very different memories. She thinks back on summer camp as a child, sleeping in old cabins. I think back to growing up in Pennsylvania when our basement would inevitably flood during a torrential downpour each summer. The same smell evokes joy for my wife and dread for me precisely because we have different histories. But as Christians we all share the same history, and so we are meant to recall the same thing as we partake of the bread and wine. They are signs meant to point away from themselves and bring our thoughts to the finished work of Christ.

But we are spiritually weak people who are prone to forget the mighty work of salvation. We may forget that it's God's work of grace and errantly conclude that it must be by our own striving. On the other hand, we might forget that it's God's work of grace *for us*. Maybe the circumstances seem too dire, our sin seems too great, and God's promises too grand. We think, *Can this so-called good news really be for me?* Both cases are signs of weak faith, and both are corrected by a proper observance of this sacrament. God graciously strengthens that faith of ours through the visible sign of the Lord's Supper. He doesn't give us a newer or better promise to counter our doubts; He gives us a better way to remember His one promise in the gospel, the greatest promise of all. It's the promise to save sinners—even the worst of sinners—through the sacrifice of His Son. He gives us a way to deepen our faith in the work of Christ that we hear preached in His word. Through the Supper God says, "Remember, salvation is from My Son, and it is for you."

We can never be told to remember too often because we are always forgetting! So remember, friends. When you see the breaking of the bread, remember the breaking of Christ's body on the cross. When you see the wine poured out, remember the blood spilt for you. When you smell the wine, remember the pleasing aroma of Christ's once-for-all sacrifice that satisfied the Father. When you taste the bread, remember that Christ is the bread from heaven that fills every spiritual need and strengthens us for our earthly pilgrimage.

Filled with Hope

The Lord's Supper is not merely about looking backward in faith to what Christ has done; it's also about *looking forward in hope* for what Christ will one day do. Often Christians take the crucial memorial aspect of the Supper and stop there, to their own hurt. Yet "the meaning of the Supper is not the sum total of our unaided powers of reflection."[6] There is so much more going on by God's power and presence when we partake of the Lord's Supper in true worship.

---

6. Waters, *Lord's Supper*, 93.

Old Covenant Foundations

A staple in old covenant ceremonial worship was the *shelamin* offering, or the peace or fellowship offering. Given only after the atonement or sin offering, we read of this in Leviticus 7. The blood would be offered to God, but the meat would be cooked and there would be a fellowship meal with both the priests and the worshipers. As Tremper Longman explains, "Functionally speaking, the *shelamin* was a religious celebration with food, a banquet, so to speak, in the presence of God himself."[7]

The practice of covenantal worship found its climax in a meal with God. Because of this, Israel understood that our great desire as people of God should be the desire to feast with God face-to-face. Consider that in Luke 14, when Jesus makes a reference to the resurrection of the dead and the end of all things, a well-informed Jew next to Him cannot help but make the connection between the end times and eating with God: "Blessed is he who shall eat bread in the kingdom of God!" (v. 15). As this guest says, true blessedness is to be able to partake of this future meal.

The guest would have good biblical precedent for drawing this conclusion. Those who knew their Old Testament well would be drawn to prophetic passages that spoke of a coming feast with Yahweh. Zephaniah says a sign that the "day of the LORD" is "at hand" is that the Lord Himself will prepare a festal sacrifice and will "[invite] His guests" (1:7). David holds out the promise that those who suffer in this life will one day be saved, writing that "the poor shall eat and be satisfied" (Ps. 22:26). Likewise, Isaiah extends an invitation to all those who are thirsty and hungry to eat freely from the bounty of Yahweh (Isa. 55:1–2).[8] Isaiah 25:6–9, however, would likely be most relevant:

---

7. Longman, *Immanuel in our Place*, 91.

8. This eschatological meal concept appears again numerous times in Revelation, confirming that this is indeed the ultimate hope of the people of God, although in Revelation details regarding the Messiah's role are given (see Rev. 3:20). Revelation 22:17 in particular harkens back to the Isaiah 55 prophecy: "And let him who thirsts come. Whoever desires, let him take the water of life freely." Most interesting is the language in 19:9, which echoes the comment of the anonymous guest in Luke 14:15: "Blessed are those who are called to the marriage supper of the Lamb!"

And in this mountain
The LORD of hosts will make for all people
A feast of choice pieces,
A feast of wines on the lees,
Of fat things full of marrow,
Of well-refined wines on the lees.
And He will destroy on this mountain
The surface of the covering cast over all people,
And the veil that is spread over all nations.
He will swallow up death forever,
And the Lord GOD will wipe away tears from all faces;
The rebuke of His people
He will take away from all the earth;
For the LORD has spoken.

And it will be said in that day:
"Behold, this is our God;
We have waited for Him, and He will save us.
This is the LORD;
We have waited for Him;
We will be glad and rejoice in His salvation."

In this passage, the blessings associated with eating bread in the kingdom of God are quite clear. It is at this meal that God will wipe away every tear, conquer His enemies, vindicate His people, and most importantly, defeat death. This "swallowing" of death is the real feast! As one writer memorably puts it, "God is preparing his own meal.... The last dish set before God is Death."[9]

For all these reasons, communing with God is not just the climax of the worship service, but it's the climax of a life of worship. That is, this divine fellowship will be the mark of our eternal blessedness. Thus the people of Israel longed for that future day of feasting. It was their great hope and expectation.

---

9. Glenn T. Miller, "Isaiah 25:6–9," *Interpretation* 49, no. 2 (April 1995): 176.

New Covenant Fulfillment

The Jews of Jesus's day often got a lot of theological matters wrong, but here was something that they got exactly right. They were meant to look forward to that grand end-times eating with God. And so when Christ instituted the Supper, He ensured that we would look forward to it as well. Though His disciples enjoyed the great pleasure and privilege of dining with Him in person, that was not the fulfillment, or consummation, of communion with God. Another feast—an eternal one—was still to come. And so Christ institutes the meal with these words, which should keep our focus on what is future: "But I say to you, I will not drink of this fruit of the vine from now on until that day when I drink it new with you in My Father's kingdom" (Matt. 26:29).

Jesus is referring to the kingdom of God in its consummated form, the kingdom as He will usher it in at the end of all things. He is referring to the new heavens and the new earth, and He promises His disciples— and us—that one that day we will feast together. Jesus blesses the bread and the wine to show we will be blessed as we partake of the Lord's Supper.[10] But ultimately this all foreshadows feasting in the consummated kingdom, where true blessedness resides: "Then he said to me, 'Write: "Blessed are those who are called to the marriage supper of the Lamb!"' And he said to me, 'These are the true sayings of God'" (Rev. 19:9).

So while there are great continuities with the old and new covenants, the new fulfills, or fills in, the old. What Old Testament Israel could know only in shadow we now can know in substance. We know that the hope of eating with God can be attained only through Christ. Jesus ensured that we would make this connection by explicitly saying at the institution of the Supper, "This is My blood of the new covenant," (Mark 14:24). This is a theologically freighted sentence that is most certainly a reference to Exodus 24:8 (the only Old Testament reference to "blood of the covenant"): "And Moses took the blood, sprinkled it on the people, and said, 'This is the blood of the covenant which the LORD has made with you according to all these words.'"

Exodus 24 is the scene of the institution of the old covenant, and we see that it is the sacrificial blood which makes the people clean and

---

10. Waters, *Lord's Supper*, 92.

fit to participate in this relationship with God. And if the people have been sprinkled with the blood, made clean and set apart, then they are granted the greatest privilege of all: communing with God. "Then Moses went up, also Aaron, Nadab, and Abihu, and seventy of the elders of Israel.... They saw God, and they ate and drank" (vv. 9, 11). But now Jesus says there's a *new* covenant instituted. There still must be sacrificial blood to constitute the relationship, but more details are given: the blood that will fulfill all those promises of God is none other than the blood of Christ.

Now having been sprinkled clean by the blood of Christ (Heb. 12:24; 1 Peter 1:2), we can eat with God. We can know for certain we will be admitted into the divine presence for that future feast which is the manifestation of all our hope and expectation. If we think the Supper is only about looking back in remembrance on the death of Christ, the sacrament will become more of a funeral than a feast. But if we see that God is pointing us forward in faith to what is to come in the next age, we will be unable to participate with anything but joy and gladness. Guy Waters writes, "If God was faithful to bring his promised Son into the world the first time to live, die, and rise again for our salvation, we can surely trust his promise that Jesus will return at the end of the age to consummate the application of his saving work in our lives."[11]

A staple in historic liturgies has helped worshipers keep this forward focus in the Supper. After partaking of the sacrament, the minister would exhort the congregation to "declare the mystery of faith." In response, they would reply, "Christ has died, Christ is risen, Christ will come again."

Joined in Love

So far we have seen that the Supper is the means by which the Lord strengthens our faith in the finished work of Christ—both looking back in remembrance on His death and looking forward in hope to His second coming. In doing so, the Supper has immediate influence on how we live in the here and now. In particular, the Supper *unites the body of Christ in the bonds of love.*

---

11. Waters, *Lord's Supper*, 91.

Looking Up

First and foremost, through the Supper we are united to the Head of the body, Christ Himself. In Paul's instructions on a well-ordered observance of the Lord's Supper in 1 Corinthians 10:16–17 he writes, "The cup of blessing which we bless, is it not the communion of the blood of Christ? The bread which we break, is it not the communion of the body of Christ? For we, though many, are one bread and one body; for we all partake of that one bread." Paul says that as we partake of this meal we are partaking of Christ. We are communing with Him, or sharing or participating in who He is and what He has done.

The Supper is a visual aid in teaching one of the central doctrines of our faith (and one of the most comforting): union with Christ. This means that when we are stirred to faith in Jesus by the Holy Spirit we are united to Him forever and ever. Union with Christ means that whatever is true of Christ is true of us. To "partake" in His blood means that His sacrifice and death count as ours. His victory over sin and death becomes ours. His payment is credited to our account. Again, how this rich element of the Supper is lost when we think of it only as a memorial meal! "Our memories of Christ are no substitute for his living presence," Marcus Peter Johnson writes. "Our recollections of Christ's death, as meaningful and enriching as they are, cannot replace our very participation in the One who was crucified."[12]

How can we say that we are united to Christ in the Supper? How can we say that we are actually fellowshipping with Him? Over the centuries this has been one of the most divisive questions in the church and perhaps remains one of the least understood. The Roman Catholic Church teaches that it must mean that bread and wine literally become the body and blood of Christ. But the Reformation corrected that notion: Christ is fully human and can be bodily present in only one place at one time. Right now He is at the right hand of God in heaven (e.g., Heb. 1:3). The Reformers believed Christ was truly present in the Supper but insisted that His presence was of a spiritual nature. *Spiritual*

---

12. Marcus Peter Johnson, *One with Christ: An Evangelical Theology of Salvation* (Wheaton, Ill.: Crossway, 2013), 240.

here means by the power of the Holy Spirit.[13] "The Holy Spirit—who unites us to Christ—lifts us up *by faith* to the heavenly places to nourish our souls upon the life-giving Christ."[14]

This corresponds with the doctrine of union with Christ. It teaches that where Christ goes we go: "But God, who is rich in mercy, because of His great love with which He loved us…raised us up together, and made us sit together in the heavenly places in Christ Jesus" (Eph. 2:4, 6). We do not bring Christ down in the Supper; He brings us up to Himself and His heavenly table. When we celebrate the Lord's Supper, it is therefore right and proper for the minister to exhort the congregation to "set your mind on things above, not on things on the earth. For you died, and your life is hidden with Christ in God" (Col. 3:2–3).

This is why it has been a common tradition since the early church in many different denominations or strands of Christianity to use the *sursum corda* in worship. *Sursum corda* is Latin for "Lift up your hearts!" Traditionally, the minister would speak these words, and the congregation would reply, "We lift them up to the Lord!" There is evidence that ministers such as Cyprian (200–258), Augustine (354–430), and Cyril of Alexandria (412–444) used the *sursum corda* in their worship services.[15] Calvin also appeals to it in his instructions for properly understanding the nature of the Lord's Supper:

> For, in order that pious souls may duly apprehend Christ in the Supper, they must be raised up to heaven…. It was established of old that before consecration the people should be told in a loud voice to lift up their hearts. Scripture itself also not only carefully recounts to us the ascension of Christ, by which he withdrew the presence of his body from our sight and company, to shake from us all carnal thinking of him, but also, whenever it recalls him,

---

13. We "really and indeed, yet not carnally and corporally [i.e., physically], but spiritually, receive and feed upon Christ crucified" in the Supper (WCF 29.7).

14. Payne, *In the Splendor of Holiness*, 96, emphasis original.

15. Jeffrey B. Wilson gives a helpful survey of this pattern in "The *Sursum Corda* Is Catholic, Part 1," *Ordained Servant Online*, October 2014, https://opc.org/os.html ?article_id=439&issue_id=98.

bids our minds be raised up, and seek him in heaven, seated at the right hand of the Father.[16]

What follows is an example of Calvin exhorting his own congregation to this end during the celebration of the Lord's Supper:

> Let us lift up our hearts and our spirits to where Jesus Christ is in the glory of his Father, and from where we await him in our redemption. And let us not waste time with these earthly and corruptible elements, which we see with our eyes and touch with our hands, seeking him there as though he were enclosed inside the bread and wine. So our souls will be inclined to be nourished and revived by his substance, when they are thus lifted above all earthly things to reach heaven and enter the kingdom of God where he dwells.[17]

Puritan John Owen once perceptively said, "One reason why we so little value the ordinance [of the Lord's Supper], and profit so little by it, may be because we understand so little of the nature of that special communion with Christ which we have therein."[18] This is exactly right and a major reason why the *sursum corda* can be helpful in worship. We need to know what is going on when we celebrate the Lord's Supper. We are communing with Christ Himself! The bread and wine are not quaint tokens commemorating a bygone era. When we receive them in faith, we are not receiving a memory of Christ; we are receiving Christ. The Belgic Confession (1561), article 35, explains this beautifully: "As certainly as we receive and hold this sacrament in our hands and eat and drink the same with our mouths, by which our life as afterwards nourished, we also do as certainly receive by faith (which is the hand and mouth of our soul) the true body and blood of Christ our only Savior in our souls, for the support of our spiritual life" (emphasis added; see also WCF 29.7).

---

16. Calvin, *Institutes*, 4.17.36.
17. As quoted in *Reformation Worship*, 328.
18. As quoted in *A Puritan Theology*, by Joel R. Beeke and Mark Jones (Grand Rapids: Reformation Heritage Books, 2012), 748.

Trust me, you don't want a mere memorial meal. Ultimately, that can do nothing for your soul—it cannot strengthen you, sustain you, or save you. You want Jesus. He is the all and all. He is the only thing that makes a bit of difference in this world. If you have Jesus, you have everything, and in the Supper you have Jesus! When we realize this, it becomes evident that if this is a meal our Lord has prepared for us and invited us to, why wouldn't we run to it every time we have the chance? "If anyone eats of this bread, he will live forever; and the bread that I shall give is My flesh, which I shall give for the life of the world" (John 6:51).

Looking Out

In the Supper we are drawn in more deeply to Christ. We are reminded that our union to Him is the deepest expression of His love for us—a love that would move Christ to "give to all the faithful his own self for heav'nly food."[19] But our communion is not only with Christ but with all those who are united to Him as well. In the previously quoted 1 Corinthians 10:16, after writing about our participation with Christ, Paul writes about our participation with the church: "For we, *though many, are...one body*; for we all partake of that one bread" (v. 17).

This meal is the great uniting work in the church. Augustine liked to refer to it as the bond of love. As we eat from the same bread, we show ourselves to be united to one another. This is the reason many congregations wait until the elements have been distributed to partake of them together, and the same reason you (hopefully) don't start eating a meal until everyone present is seated at the table. We wait to eat together because it's a family meal. As the Lord's Supper brings us to Christ, it also brings us to one another. We are united as one family—one body. Again, the Supper presents for us a visible demonstration of an invisible reality: the Holy Spirit is at work within all of us, bringing us together into deeper conformity to Christ.

Calvin writes this: "For the Lord so communicates his body to us there that he is made completely one with us and we with him. Now, since he has only one body, of which he makes us all partakers, it is

---

19. Gerard Moultrie, adapter, "Let All Mortal Flesh Keep Silence" (1864), in *Trinity Hymnal.*

necessary that all of us also be made one body by such participation."[20] We who are many become one in Christ, for we have the one Spirit. Any and all dividing differences are set aside and we come together in solidarity under the Head of the body, who is Christ. We partake together as a sign of unconditional and selfless love that has been poured into our hearts by Christ and now pours forth into each other's lives. In the Supper, we learn "that we cannot love Christ without loving him in the brethren."[21]

To miss this outward-facing aspect of the Supper is to miss the Supper. Paul says if we partake of the meal in a selfish way, we haven't truly fed on Christ: "Therefore when you come together in one place, it is not to eat the Lord's Supper. For in eating, each one takes his own supper ahead of others; and one is hungry and another is drunk. What! Do you not have houses to eat and drink in? Or do you despise the church of God and shame those who have nothing? What shall I say to you? Shall I praise you in this? I do not praise you" (1 Cor. 11:20–22). We show our union with the selfless, sacrificial Christ when we selflessly and sacrificially commune with His people.

God's Provision in the Wilderness
Life for ancient Israel was truly one of wilderness wanderings. On account of this they often grumbled and complained. They would much rather return to Egypt where they at least got four square meals a day. So we read in Psalm 78,

> But they sinned even more against Him
> By rebelling against the Most High in the wilderness.
> And they tested God in their heart
> By asking for the food of their fancy.
> Yes, they spoke against God:
> They said, "Can God prepare a table in the wilderness?
> Behold, He struck the rock,
> So that the waters gushed out,
> And the streams overflowed.

20. Calvin, *Institutes*, 4.17.38.
21. Calvin, *Institutes*, 4.17.38.

Can He give bread also?
Can He provide meat for His people?" (vv. 17–20)

The answer, as we know, was (and is) yes. Not only could God give bread but He did. God provides in the wilderness. He is a sustaining God. He gave to Israel water from the rock and bread from heaven. He sent the ravens to feed Elijah when he was cast out into the desert. And because of all this, David can rightly say that "You prepare a table before me in the presence of my enemies" (Ps. 23:5). These were all pictures to remind God's people that if He could provide in the worst of physical circumstances, then He could certainly provide spiritually.

This is what we get in the Lord's Supper: God sustaining our weak faith through our wilderness wandering—sustaining us on our journey from here to the true promised land. It's like a bit of heaven come to earth (although, really, it's like earth has gone up to heaven). The point is this: in the communing aspect of worship, God strengthens our faith by giving us a taste of that future promise of eternal fellowship with Him. What the Israelites longed for as they read passages like Isaiah 25 we get in the here and now. The Supper is literally a taste of the final feast in heaven, what Revelation calls the marriage supper of the Lamb, the guests of which are those who are truly blessed (Rev. 19:9).

So think of this the next time you come to the Table: this is God's greatest sign to you that you belong to Him. We commune with God today in the Lord's Supper as a sure sign that we will commune with Him on that last day and for eternity. In the story of worship that God is telling, He calls us, cleanses us, and consecrates us all so that we would belong to Him. Then He gives us proof that we truly do: He invites us to sit down and have a meal with Him.

Discussion Questions

1. In what ways does the Lord's Supper strengthen our (1) faith, (2) hope, and (3) love?

2. Is the Lord's Supper merely a memorial meal? Why or why not?

3. What does Isaiah 25 teach us about the hope of the end times?

4. How is Christ present in the Supper?

5. How does this understanding challenge the way you view the Lord's Supper in worship?

Chapter 12

We Get a New Name

How sweet the name of Jesus sounds
In a believer's ear!
It soothes his sorrows, heals his wounds,
And drives away his fear.

—John Newton

At some point in your schooling, you have probably come across the handy diagram that explains the various components of a strong, dramatic narrative. It's a little line that begins steadily with the exposition, takes a vicious turn skyward with the conflict and rising action, reaches its peak with the climax, and then gently descends with the falling action and denouement. In the worship service, the blessing and sending are like the denouement. We are coming off the mountain of the Lord where we have eaten with God Himself (Isa. 25:6). As we come to the conclusion of our meeting with God, we receive a blessing, or a benediction.

What exactly is the benediction? The benediction is not simply a way to close the service. It's not a final prayer. It's not a simple farewell—a way to say "goodbye, come back next time." Nor is it simply a "good word" from the pastor to the congregation, as perhaps you may have heard it explained in the past.[1] It is far more than that. *In the benediction,*

---

1. For example, R. Kent Hughes writes, "A benediction is simply a 'good word' prayed by the pastor at the conclusion of a worship service." As we will see, the benediction is not "simply a 'good word,'" nor is it a prayer *to* God as much as it is a proclamation *from* God. *The Pastor's Book* (Wheaton, Ill.: Crossway, 2015), 309.

*God blesses His people by confirming that His name is on them for good
in Christ, and thereby strengthens them to serve Him in the week ahead.*

Benedictions in Scripture

Perhaps the most popular benediction in all of Scripture is what is
known as the Aaronic blessing in Numbers 6:22–27:

> And the LORD spoke to Moses, saying: "Speak to Aaron and his
> sons, saying, 'This is the way you shall bless the children of Israel.
> Say to them:
>
> > "The LORD bless you and keep you;
> > The LORD make His face shine upon you,
> > And be gracious to you;
> > The LORD lift up His countenance upon you,
> > And give you peace."'
>
> "So they shall put My name on the children of Israel, and I will
> bless them."

In this benediction (and others) we see that God's good favor and
pleasure are said to rest on His people. This would continue to be a part
of covenantal worship in both the Old and the New Testaments. Many
new covenant benedictions show up at the close of letters or sermons
that were meant to be read publicly in the church's worship service:

> Now may the God of hope fill you with all joy and peace in
> believing, that you may abound in hope by the power of the Holy
> Spirit. (Rom. 15:13)

> The grace of the Lord Jesus Christ, and the love of God, and the
> communion of the Holy Spirit be with you all. (2 Cor. 13:14)

> Now may the God of peace who brought up our Lord Jesus from
> the dead, that great Shepherd of the sheep, through the blood of
> the everlasting covenant, make you complete in every good work
> to do His will, working in you what is well pleasing in His sight,
> through Jesus Christ, to whom be glory forever and ever. Amen.
> (Heb. 13:20–21)

> But may the God of all grace, who called us to His eternal glory

by Christ Jesus, after you have suffered a while, perfect, establish, strengthen, and settle you. To Him be the glory and the dominion forever and ever. Amen. (1 Peter 5:10–11)

Perhaps most important of all is that God concludes His entire book of special revelation with a blessing: "The grace of our Lord Jesus Christ be with you all. Amen" (Rev. 22:21).

In both old and new covenantal settings, we also find that the method of bestowing God's blessing is through the words of a priest spoken while his hands are raised. In Leviticus 9:22 we read, "Then Aaron lifted his hand toward the people, blessed them, and came down from offering the sin offering, the burnt offering, and peace offerings." Likewise, in Luke 24:50 we find Jesus doing the same thing for His disciples: "And He led them out as far as Bethany, and He lifted up His hands and blessed them."

It is evident that it was the practice of both the first high priest and the Great High Priest to raise their hands when they blessed their respective congregations. What is the significance of this? Hand-raising represents the practice of laying on of hands. Obviously you cannot lay hands on every person when you have a large group, so raising the hands in the air with palms toward the people represents laying on of hands. And in Scripture, when hands are laid on in God's service, it is a sign of *transference*. We have at least two examples of this. On the Day of Atonement, the priest would lay his hand on the scapegoat, and this would represent the transference of the sin of the people from the priest to the animal. In the New Testament, we read that men are set apart for ordained leadership in the church by the laying on of hands (1 Tim. 4:14). This symbolizes the transference of God's grace and power from one ordained leader to the next. In the benediction, God confers His saving grace to His people through the means of the minister.

No Other Name

If we go back and look more closely at that Aaronic benediction, we find something quite puzzling at the end. God says that in pronouncing the blessing, priests will "put My name on the children of Israel, and I will bless them" (Num. 6:27). This summarizes for us in what way we receive God's blessings: precisely by receiving His name. It is hard to explain the theology behind names in Scripture, but in essence everything that made a person who they were was believed to be packed into their name. If you knew a person's name, you really *knew* them. You knew what they were about, what made them tick, what their weaknesses and strengths were. In terms of deities, it was thought that if you knew the deity's name, you could master it. This is likely why Jacob wants to know the name of the angel with whom he is wrestling (Gen. 32:28–29).

Throughout Scripture we see that God is zealous to maintain the honor of His name, for His name is who He is (Ex. 20:7). His name holds within itself His divine character and attributes. Remember the scene with Moses at the burning bush?

> Then Moses said to God, "Indeed, when I come to the children of Israel and say to them, "The God of your fathers has sent me to you," and they say to me, "What is His name?" what shall I say to them?"
>
> And God said to Moses, "I AM WHO I AM." And He said, "Thus you shall say to the children of Israel, 'I AM has sent me to you.'" Moreover God said to Moses, "Thus you shall say to the children of Israel: 'The LORD God of your fathers, the God of Abraham, the God of Isaac, and the God of Jacob, has sent me to you. This is My name forever, and this is My memorial to all generations.'" (Ex. 3:13–15)

In this passage God attributes His name to both His characteristic of faithfulness and His attributes of eternality, omnipotence, and independence. Later on in the life of Moses, his greatest blessing this side of heaven is when God says He will pass before him and proclaim His name "the LORD" to him (Ex. 33:19). During the days of David and Solomon, God established a temple for His name (1 Kings 5:5), and later He puts His "name there forever" (1 Kings 9:3). In the Psalms God promises to protect and deliver the one who knows His name (9:10; 91:14). God is so zealous about maintaining the holiness that is His name that He threatens the death penalty for anyone who would profane it (Lev. 24:16).[2]

And yet it is this very name that God gives to us in the benediction. This name is so marvelous, so majestic, so holy and sacred, yet He gives it to us frail and feeble creatures. Hughes Oliphant Old writes, "[The benediction is] a blessing that seals the Church in the name of the Lord. In giving us His name He brings us into His care and gives us a share in the household of faith."[3]

Is there any greater comfort or assurance than knowing we share God's name? When we belong to Christ we have that name "Christian" stamped on our hearts, and God will indeed save the one who knows, or who bears, His name. It's a way of differentiating. The heathens and the ungodly of this world do not receive God's benediction. Only those who by faith come into the house of worship receive God's blessing, and therefore God can look out over the world and say, "Who has My name?" Those who have His name have Him and therefore have salvation.

All week the world around us gives us a name. Maybe the name is "fat" or "rich" or "smart" or "funny" or "not good enough" or "not as bad as that guy" or whatever. The world is feeding us lies: telling us who we are, who we should be, and what matters most. And yet a grand and glorious purpose of worship is to wash that away and give us a different—and proper—view and outlook on everything, including ourselves. A major point of the worship service is to teach us who we really are: those who are called by God out of sin, cleansed by His gospel and freely forgiven, led by His word, and invited to feast with Him at an eternal meal. And if all that doesn't reorient us entirely, if that doesn't teach us that we belong to Christ and not to our sin, then God does this one final thing: He gives us His name.

Benedictions and Baptism

It's important to note that the benediction is not the first time that Christians receive the name of God placed on them in the worship

---

2. Incidentally, this is what began the tradition of Jews refusing to use the name YHWH in speech.

3. As quoted in Payne, *In the Splendor of Holiness*, 103.

service. In fact, the very initiation into the worship service is when they first receive God's covenant name: at baptism. Baptism is the admission into the visible church, the entrance into the worshiping community; and according to Jesus's own instruction, when individuals are baptized they are to receive nothing less than the name of God: "Go therefore and make disciples of all the nations, baptizing them *in the name* of the Father and of the Son and of the Holy Spirit" (Matt. 28:19).

"In the name" does not mean simply "by the authority of," though it certainly means that. But it would perhaps be better rendered "*into* the name" (as in the American Standard Version and other Bible translations). What does this mean? In his superb work on Christian baptism, theologian J. V. Fesko explains that "the person who is baptized into a name or person is baptized into a relationship…. 'Baptized into' is a way of expressing the idea that a person is 'in union with' the person or name into which he has been baptized."[4] When we are baptized, we are brought into the covenant name of God Himself, and when the Holy Spirit works saving faith in our hearts, we receive all the blessings that come along with that. This is what it takes to worship properly; we must belong to God—we must have that uniting relationship to Him—so it is fitting that baptism is the initiatory rite into the church and into a life of worship. Now that we have God's name on us, we are part of His family. When joined with Spirit-wrought faith, we can really and truly call God our Father and His Son our brother. We share their family name. And because we belong to the family, we can come into the family house and worship.

Though baptism is a one-time event, through the benediction God continually reminds us of the promises that were sealed to us in our baptism. We can easily forget about the ongoing significance of baptism, and for this reason a previous generation of Christians used to speak about "improving your baptism." Their concern was that we continue to remind ourselves of what God has promised us in baptism and also remember that we now belong to Him and must live for Him. The Westminster Larger Catechism 167 says one of the ways we can improve

---

4. J. V. Fesko, *Word, Water, and Spirit* (Grand Rapids: Reformation Heritage Books, 2010), 311.

our baptism is "by drawing strength from the death and resurrection of Christ, into whom we are baptized, for the mortifying of sin, and quickening of grace." In other words, one of the ways we improve our baptism is by remembering that we are united to Christ. We are now defined by Him—not by our sins or shortcomings but by all Christ's perfections and the blessings we receive because of them.

Therefore, hearing and receiving by faith the benediction at the close of a service is one of the great ways to improve our baptism. When God pronounces His blessing on us through the minister, it's the same blessing we received in baptism. The blessing we received as we first entered the church's worship is the same blessing we hear every week as we exit. God is reminding us that we belong to Him—and that we have His name on us. Forever.

So Send I You

We do not receive God's immense blessings to hoard them to ourselves, like some miser. God blesses us in order to strengthen us for the week ahead, for the work ahead—that is, for the gospel work that is ahead of us. If worship is about showing us who we are in Christ, then we will see that it comes with a calling, or a task. Just as there was a task for the very first humans, redeemed humanity has one as well. Smith writes, "The end of worship is bound up with the end of being human. In other words, the point of *worship* is bound up with the point of *creation*. The goal of Christian worship is a renewal of the mandate in creation: to be (re)made in God's image and then *sent* as his image bearers *to* and *for* the world."[5]

We still have work to do. But what God calls us to He equips us for. Bryan Chapell explains, "The benediction is the promise of blessing for the tasks God calls his people to do"; thus it "is often followed by a charge (e.g., 'Go in peace,' or 'Go now and serve God in this way with confidence that He goes with you to help you and to bless you')."[6]

---

5. Smith, *You Are What You Love,* 88, emphasis original.
6. Bryan Chapell, *Christ-Centered Worship: Letting the Gospel Shape Our Practice* (Grand Rapids: Baker Academic, 2009), 254. I appreciated one church's liturgy (Grace and Peace Presbyterian Church, California, Maryland), which ended with the benediction; however, this was followed by "the dismissal," wherein the printed bulletin signified

Is this not a fitting conclusion to the story of worship that God has just told us? It really means that the story is not over yet. It means "Tune in for next week…." But even so, in this break in between, we truly go with God. We go with His name—the blessing that will bolster us to accomplish the commission He gives us. And though this benediction and commission are spoken by a minister, they are the very words of God. This reminds us that it is the mighty God, Creator of the universe and Redeemer through Jesus Christ, who is telling the story. He calls us in, and He sends us out. He gets the first word, and He gets the very last. And each word is one of grace.

Discussion Questions

1. What is a benediction?

2. In the Bible, who would give benedictions?

3. What is the connection between a blessing from God and our identity in Christ?

4. What role does baptism play in the worship service? What is the connection between baptisms and benedictions?

5. How should receiving this blessing from God simultaneously act as a commission from Him?

---

that while "gathered worship has ended, service to Christ continues." The minister then declared, "Let us go forth to love and serve the Lord," with a response from the congregation: "Thanks be to God!"

Chapter 13

We Sing a New Song

The good news of Christ's great deliverance
tunes the heart to sing.
—Martin Luther

Americans—and all Westerners, really—no longer sing as a community. There was a time not too long ago in the history of our culture when it would have been perfectly commonplace to sing at parties, neighborhood gatherings, or with a few close friends around the table after dinner. But in the past several decades, this practice has receded into such obscurity that it has almost become extinct. Singing has been regulated to the safe and solitary confines of the shower or the car on the daily commute.

Think about it: outside of a religious setting, when was the last time you joined your voices in song with a group of friends and strangers? By my recollection, the last two times I experienced something like that were at Petco Park in San Diego. The first was joining with thousands of Padres fans singing "Take Me Out to the Ball Game" during the seventh inning stretch—a welcome diversion to the fact that the Philadelphia Phillies were crushing them. The second was singing along with even more fans to Billy Joel's classic hits as he performed a sold-out show one summer evening.

It seems like ball games, concerts, and certain nationalistic events that could stir a group to sing the national anthem or "My Country, 'Tis of Thee" are the only things strong enough to pry open our society's vocal cords to let out a unified sound. We no longer sing together. "The reasons why are legion," journalist Karen Loew writes in an article for *The Atlantic* on the disappearance of communal singing. "We are insecure about our voices. We don't know the words. We resent being forced into an activity together. We feel uncool. And since we're out of practice as a society, the person who dares to begin a song risks having no one join her."[1]

This means that to our culture, unabashed communal singing is perhaps the most surprising aspect of Christian worship. There's nothing quite like it: a place where people willingly sing together—even if their voices aren't all that great! A member of my church once brought her unchurched friend to a service. Afterward, she asked her friend what she thought of the service, and the reply was something like, "What was up with all the singing?"

What is up with it? Why do we do it, and why so much of it? Singing is unfamiliar in our day, and yet God has commanded it of His church. He has created us to be a society of song. So we need to know what we're doing when we sing on Sundays. We need to learn what is happening when we worship through song. It is not as simplistic as our culture would make it—that is, done for entertainment or out of nationalist gusto. Rather, God has gifted us with song that we might have *a fitting way to praise Him for His work, pray to Him with our deepest needs, and proclaim to one another the sanctifying truths of the gospel.*[2]

Melody with Meaning

First, we must recognize that all our singing is rooted in the work of our Savior, Jesus Christ. If we don't understand this, we have failed to offer up acceptable worship to God in the area of song. Worshipful singing is not constituted by any emotional thrill we might get from the music, but rather it comes from understanding why God is worthy of our song. And He is worthy because of the redemption we have through Jesus

---

1. Karen Loew, "How Communal Singing Disappeared from American Life," *The Atlantic*, March 28, 2012, https://www.theatlantic.com/entertainment/archive/2012/03/how-communal-singing-disappeared-from-american-life/255094/.

2. I am indebted to Paul S. Jones for this categorization. He writes that "music properly fulfills three roles in the context of worship: praise, prayer, and proclamation." For a more expansive treatment on the role of music and singing in worship, I highly recommend his book *What Is Worship Music?* (Phillipsburg, N.J.: P&R, 2010).

Christ. So God is not pleased with mere music, but music and voice that are lifted up to Him with purpose in response to the gift of the gospel. Shakespeare's Hamlet once lamented, "My words fly up, my thoughts remain below; words without thoughts never to heaven go!"[3] Sadly, many sanctuaries are filled with sound that doesn't rise above the ceiling simply because people are singing thoughtlessly or singing words that are not properly rooted in God's Word. So Paul lays out the pattern for acceptable singing when he writes, "I will sing with the spirit, and I will also sing with the understanding" (1 Cor. 14:15).

God has always expected the sounds of worship to be an echo of His mighty acts in, through, and for His people. Consider that in the Psalms—the greatest of songbooks for covenant worshipers—we are repeatedly commanded not only to sing but specifically to sing a "new song" (Pss. 33:3; 40:3; 96:1; 98:1; 144:9; 149:1). Old Testament scholar Tremper Longman III points out that the references to a "new song" in Scripture come in the context of warfare: "A new song is a hymn of victory, sung after God has made all things new by his defeat of the forces of evil."[4] And what is the mightiest act of all that God has accomplished? What is the greatest victory that He has won? It is, in the famous words of John Owen, "the death of death in the death of Christ."

It is the victory of the empty tomb that informs and inspires all our songs. There is no part of worship, of meeting with God, that is possible apart from the work of Christ, and this includes our singing. It is Jesus who makes us a new creation. It is Jesus who one day will bring a new heavens and a new earth. And it is Jesus who gives us a new song. We can turn our ear up to heaven, as it were, and hear that the eternal choir gets this reality. As John tells us,

> They sang a new song, saying,
> "You are worthy to take the scroll,
> And to open its seals;
> For You were slain,
> And have redeemed us to God by Your blood
> Out of every tribe and tongue and people and nation,

---

3. William Shakespeare, *Hamlet, Prince of Denmark*, act 3, scene 4, lines 100–101.
4. Tremper Longman III, *Psalms* (Downers Grove, Ill.: InterVarsity, 2014), 166.

> And have made us kings and priests to our God;
> And we shall reign on the earth." (Rev. 5:9–10)

Christ is the content of the songs of heaven. He ought to be the content of our songs on earth. He is the reason we are commanded to sing a new song. So whether we are praising God for what He has done, praying to Him in our trouble, or proclaiming the truth of the Bible, every song is possible only because Jesus has made it so. Let's explore how.

Praise

In ancient Israel, "the usual way to approach Zion was with hymns of praise."[5] Is it not fitting that as we enter the heavenly Mount Zion in Christian worship that a song be on our lips as well? Praise, according to Hughes Oliphant Old, is "the sense of awe and wonder we have when we enter the presence of God."[6] As long as we are present with our awesome God, praise is inevitable (Matt. 9:15). That's why singing is appropriately punctuated throughout the entirety of the worship service and not just grouped together in a half-hour segment at the beginning, middle, or end. As we are before God and amazed by His glory, grace, and goodness, we cannot help but sing. Singing is the overflow of the soul. It is the outlet for our most ardent emotions. For these reasons, singing is truly good for us.

Some may protest that the God of the Bible is a narcissist with His countless commands that we praise Him—a God so consumed with Himself that He could not possibly be concerned for us. This was an initial stumbling block for the great apologist C. S. Lewis as he came to the faith. He writes in *Reflections on the Psalms* that at first it seemed ridiculous: "the demand so clamorously made by all religious people that we should 'praise' God; still more in the suggestion that God Himself demanded it. We all despise the man who demands continued assurance of his own virtue," yet this is precisely what Lewis thought God was doing. To him, those portions in Scripture where God commanded

---

5. Old, *Worship: Reformed according to Scripture*, 34.
6. Old, *Worship: Reformed according to Scripture*, 34.

praise were "hideously like [God] saying, 'What I most want is to be told that I am good and great.'"[7]

Granted, it would be sinful of God to demand worship if He were not worthy. But He is worthy, and this fact demands that we praise Him. He is, in the truest sense of the word, praiseworthy. But as with all God's commands, He instructs us to do only that which is good and right for us. So it's not that God selfishly or cruelly demands praise of us but rather that He calls us into the activity that will complete our joy. In fact, to not praise God would mean we have missed out on something. Lewis grew to understand that to not "appreciate [God] is to have lost the greatest experience, and in the end to have lost all."[8] And so praise is both a demand from God and a delight for us. Lewis concludes, "I think we delight to praise what we enjoy because the praise not merely expresses but completes the enjoyment; it is its appointed consummation."[9] God gives the command to praise Him, but true worshipers rightly respond, "It is good to give thanks to the LORD, and to sing praises to Your name, O Most High" (Ps. 92:1).

As I have said, the whole of worship ought to be filled with praise and acclamation. We rightly praise God as He calls us into worship, as He pardons us of our sin, as He illuminates our hearts and minds with the word, as He invites us to His heavenly table, and as He blesses us with His high and holy name. All these things He has done for us in Christ, and so it is fitting that it is "through him that we utter our Amen to God" (2 Cor. 1:20 ESV). Put another way, Christ is the content of our song. And with the perfections of Christ's person and work at the center, nothing short of joyous praise can appropriately mark the songs and the singing of worshiping saints. In the words of Isaac Watts,

> Let those refuse to sing
> that never knew our God;
> but children of the heav'nly King
> may speak their joys abroad.[10]

---

7. C. S. Lewis, *Reflection on the Psalms* (San Francisco: HarperCollins, 2017), 105–6.
8. Lewis, *Reflection on the Psalms*, 108.
9. Lewis, *Reflection on the Psalms*, 111.
10. Isaac Watts, "Come, We That Love the Lord" (1707), in *Trinity Hymnal*.

Prayer

Insofar as prayer is any type of direct address to God, corporate singing in worship falls under this category. John Calvin recognized the role of singing as prayer. In the introduction to the 1543 Genevan Psalter he writes, "As for public prayers, there are two kinds: the one consists simply of speech, the other of song." Or there's the oft-quoted aphorism that "the man who sings prays twice."

But even when prayer is viewed more narrowly, in terms of petition and supplication, singing plays an important function. This idea of sung prayer and petition pushes back against a trend in mainstream evangelicalism of employing exclusively upbeat and joyful songs in worship. Indeed, as I previously noted, joyous praise should be the predominant mark of our singing since it should be the predominant mark of the Christian (Phil. 4:4). But it need not and should not be the only thing that defines our singing. Life does not always play out in a major key, so why should our songs? This tends to be more of an issue in those striving after an entertainment aesthetic in worship—after all, what is entertaining about sin, calamity, or distress? If we plan worship with consumers and not Christians in mind, then human wisdom will balk at the thought of addressing such raw and vulnerable issues in church. But life is difficult and messy, and God wants us to come and cast our cares before Him. Moreover, church singing offers a cathartic forum for us to express our deepest troubles without having to pretend like everything in life is A-OK. As my dear friend has strikingly put it, limiting church from becoming an exercise in entertainment is really "the liberation of our whole selves and experiences before God. All that hippy praise music can be stifling."[11]

The heavy concentration of songs of lament and distress in the Psalms shows that it is appropriate to come to God with our troubles, concerns, problems, and worries—and not just to come to Him, but to come to Him in song. Paul and Silas knew that singing was a powerful way to appeal to God and comfort one another in their trial in the Philippian jail (Acts 16:25). The Psalter gives us a proper balance of emotive music: songs of praise as well as lament, songs of adoration

---

11. Luke Sayers, personal correspondence, October 22, 2019. Used with permission.

as well as confession. Handling these more sensitive subjects can seem awkward at times, but when we look to the Psalms, we know the appropriate way to do it.

The best of Christian hymnody has taken its cue from the balanced emotions of the Psalms. Tragedy has often been put to music. Failing health moved Henry F. Lyte to compose "Abide with Me," and the sudden loss of family at sea inspired "It Is Well with My Soul" by Horatio G. Spafford. These songs and others have been helpful not only for the original authors but also for countless Christians in subsequent generations facing similar hardship. I am not advocating for bare sentimentality but rather for scriptural imagery and language to be put to use by God's people in time of need. The church's singing should teach Christians how to pray. It should serve as a lesson in how to cry out to God: "Let Your ears be attentive to the voice of my supplications" (Ps. 130:2).

This reminds us that when we sing in corporate worship, it is part of the covenant conversation in which we speak back to God. And we know that when we call out to Him, whether speaking or singing, He hears us for the sake of Christ (Rom. 8:34; 1 John 5:14–15). Christ is the Mediator who makes our cares His own and brings them to the throne of the heavenly Father. Our prayers become His. Our requests and petitions are made by Him. As our Great High Priest, He sings our humble song into the Father's ear, and therefore we can know that we are heard.

Proclamation

While singing is primarily speaking to God, we can't discount that it can also simultaneously be a means of proclaiming God's truth to one another. This is what the apostle Paul teaches us about the role of singing in worship when he instructs the Colossian church to "let the word of Christ dwell in you richly in all wisdom, teaching and admonishing one another in psalms and hymns and spiritual songs, singing with grace in your hearts to the Lord" (Col. 3:16). Notice how he parallels "teaching and admonishing" with "singing." Congregational singing acts as a sort of communal preaching. In Colossians Paul says singing allows the "word of Christ" to dwell in us. This is a synonym for the gospel. It's the same phrase he uses in Romans 10:17: "So faith comes from hearing, and hearing through the word of Christ" (ESV). Singing is a means by which faith in the gospel is planted and cultivated in our hearts.

In some respects music can be a more effective communicator of God's truth than any other medium because of the ease with which it can be memorized. Martin Luther wrote, "Music and notes, which are wonderful gifts and creations of God, do help gain a better understanding of the text, especially when sung by a congregation and sung earnestly.... We are made better and stronger in faith when his holy Word is impressed on our hearts by sweet music."[12] His opponents knew this to be the case as well. One Jesuit wrote, "Luther has murdered more souls with his songs than with his writings and sermons."[13]

This reminds us that while it is good and right to sing praise to the Lord at all times, it is especially necessary that we sing when we are gathered with the saints. Psalm 149:1 reminds us that the main venue for godly praise is not in the shower or in the car or in our prayer closets, but in the church:

> Praise the LORD!
> Sing to the LORD a new song,
> And His praise in the assembly of saints.

Similarly, as one psalter setting of Psalm 22 puts it, "Amid the thronging worshipers Jehovah will I bless" (cf. 22:22). Singing is part of corporate worship because it shares in that crucial work of the ministry of the word: teaching God's soul-saving truth to God's people.

This means that when we sing we are not just communicating to God or even communicating with one another, though we are certainly doing those things. But singing is a responsibility, a duty. When we sing God's word we ought to realize that God is using this moment to manifest His glory and splendor and, indeed, His gospel to those who are present. Puritan Thomas Adams said that in praise we cannot add to God's glory or detract from it. God is all-glorious by His nature. But "we that cannot make his name greater can make it seem greater; and

12. As quoted in Paul S. Jones, *Singing and Making Music: Issues in Church Music Today* (Phillipsburg, N.J.: P&R, 2006), 3–4, emphasis added.
13. As quoted in Paul Nettl, *Luther and Music* (Philadelphia: Muhlenberg Press, 1948), 49.

though we cannot enlarge his glory, we can enlarge the manifestation of his glory."[14] We have a responsibility, then, "before God and these witnesses" to sing with meaning and conviction and passion, no matter our musical ability in the eyes of the world. In the preface of the original United Methodist Hymnal, titled *Select Hymns* (1761), John Wesley gave worshipers the following instruction:

> Beware of singing as if you were half dead, or half asleep; but lift up your voice with strength. Be no more afraid of your voice now, nor more ashamed of its being heard, than when you sung the songs of Satan.... Have an eye to God in every word you sing. Aim at pleasing him more than yourself, or any other creature.... So shall your singing be such as the Lord will approve of here, and reward when he cometh in the clouds of heaven.

Let Us Love and Sing and Wonder

Are you in awe of the gospel? Are you in love with the Lord Jesus Christ? Then you will sing. We sing not only because we are commanded to sing but because the person and work of our triune God compels us to sing. We sing because we cannot be silent, to borrow the language of an old hymn.[15] German minister and martyr Dietrich Bonhoeffer wrote that "the heart sings because it is overflowing with Christ."[16]

If the word of Christ is dwelling richly within you, you will be unable to do anything but sing. Therefore it is paramount that our songs be filled with the word—and nothing but the word. Word-centered song will produce a people who are word-centered. Songs based on and filled with Scripture are songs that are Godward, not manward; Christ-focused, not self-indulgent; grounded in objectivity, not aimlessly floating in subjectivity. The overemphasis we find in many churches today on feelings and emotions in worship is destructive to the formation of godly character. The sad reality is that many Christians

---

14. As quoted in Malcolm H. Watts, "The Case for Psalmody, with Some Reference to the Psalter's Sufficiency for Christian Worship," in *Sing a New Song*, ed. Joel R. Beeke and Anthony T. Selvaggio (Grand Rapids: Reformation Heritage Books, 2010), 124.

15. Fanny Crosby, "Redeemed! How I Love to Proclaim It!" (1882), in *Trinity Hymnal*.

16. Dietrich Bonhoeffer, *Life Together* (New York: HarperOne, 1954), 58.

evaluate the merit of a worship service based on the emotional thrill they get from the music. This is dangerous; if we say true worship happens when we feel good, then we impress on the hearts of worshipers that anything which feels good is therefore true. Marva Dawn reminds us that "our goal is that worship practices will form character so that believers respond to God with commitment, love, thought, and virtuous action. The Scriptures make it clear that God wants his people not just to feel good, but to be good." So she warns, "Shallow music forms shallow people."[17]

God wants our song not because He wants the sound but because He wants our souls. Our song is a sign that our hearts have been utterly transfixed on Christ and transformed by Him. So we sing not primarily with the vocal cords or lips but with our hearts. Is your heart singing in worship? Bonhoeffer goes on: "Where the heart is not singing there is no melody, there is only the dreadful medley of human self-praise. Where the singing is not to the Lord, it is singing to the honor of the self or the music, and the new song becomes a song to idols."[18]

So we must be cautious not to be carried away by the music or the song in worship, which many churches today think is the equivalent of an authentic, meaningful worship "experience." Rather, we want to be carried away by the *new* song—that is, by the redemption accomplished for us in the victory of Christ over sin and death. It's the victory that makes worship possible. It's the victory that makes entrance into God's presence possible. And so it is this new song that best expresses the supernatural wonder of worship. It is the worthy Lamb who makes us worthy to be priests before God, a people who offer themselves up as a living sacrifice: a people who are called out of the world and into His presence; a people who receive His word and respond in faith and obedience; a people who fellowship and feast with Him; a people who are sent to the world as ambassadors and witnesses.

In a word, it is the new song that consecrates us as a people who worship.

---

17. Dawn, *Reaching Out without Dumbing Down*, 175.
18. Bonhoeffer, *Life Together*, 58–59.

Discussion Questions

1. What does it mean to "sing a new song"?

2. Is it narcissistic of God to command us to praise Him? Why or why not?

3. How is singing a responsibility of Christians in a corporate worship setting?

4. What are some ways we can avoid the danger of being carried along by the music and singing, as opposed to allowing the music and singing to carry us to Christ?

5. How does singing best express the supernatural wonder of worship?

PART 3:
Preparing Our Hearts

Chapter 14

Extraordinarily Ordinary Worship

God has chosen the foolish things of the world to put to shame the wise, and God has chosen the weak things of the world to put to shame the things which are mighty; and the base things of the world and the things which are despised God has chosen, and the things which are not, to bring to nothing the things that are, that no flesh should glory in His presence.
—the apostle Paul, 1 Corinthians 1:27–29

"Work on their horror of the Same Old Thing."[1] That was Master Screwtape's advice to his nephew and demon-in-training Wormwood, captured in C. S. Lewis's imaginative work *The Screwtape Letters*. To steer people clear of the Christian faith, let them see it as boring and tedious, Screwtape says. Let them become distracted with things that seem more important, more exciting, more meaningful. This, apparently, is what the devils are up to.

Do you know that horror of the Same Old Thing? I think we know it more today than when Lewis wrote back in the mid-twentieth century. Can you admit that your life is, at least at times, boring and normal? Can you recognize that most days for most people are quite unremarkable? That can be really terrifying to people. They want to leave a mark. They want to have made a difference.

Social media thrives off of people's fears of the Same Old Thing, and thus we strive to make sure our lives seem epic and awesome. We rarely ever post or share online about the everyday ordinariness of our

---

1. C. S. Lewis, *The Screwtape Letters* (San Francisco: HarperCollins, 2001), 135.

lives since that would be giving away the secret that our lives are just that: ordinary! We feel compelled to maintain the myth and keep up the image, so we make sure people see we are always having fun, going cool places, hanging with cool friends—anything as long as it's not the Same Old Thing.

Interestingly, sharing your ordinary life with the rest of a world that is just as ordinary as yours is considered so brave and bold that it actually has to be pointed out. Pictures are now captioned "no filter"—just so people can know that even your untouched, unadulterated boring life isn't really boring after all. Similarly, people are applauded for posting photos of themselves without makeup on as a sign of authenticity and vulnerability. But we wouldn't get applauded for going out in public in our workout clothes—that would be absurd. It's just normal life after all. What is happening on social media, interestingly enough, is people desperately trying to stretch their ordinary, normal life into something noteworthy.

Michael Horton says that "'ordinary' has to be one of the loneliest words in our vocabulary today," and he is absolutely right.[2] No one wants to own it. No one wants to be associated with it. To do so would be tantamount to being branded with a scarlet O. But here's the problem for twenty-first-century Christians: by God's design, "ordinary" is inherent to worship. True worship is not epic or awesome, not at least in the sense that we tend to use those words today. It is meant to be fairly unremarkable: centered on a book, a table, and water. Nothing flashy there. That means we could easily fall prey to the horror of the Same Old Thing in worship, and indeed many have. Worship leaders have long sought innovations and inventions to keep people hooked and interested. A better approach, I would posit, is by happily owning God's ordinary methods, readying our discontented hearts for what God has in store for us, and learning to love His ways. To that end, in this chapter I want to explore in what ways God has established worship to be ordinary. This way we know what we are expecting and are less likely to be deterred by the Same Old Thing. But more than that, I

---

2. Horton, *Ordinary*, 11.

want us to see how these seemingly ordinary aspects of worship, by the Spirit and through faith, are used by God for truly extraordinary ends.

Ordinary

Let's pull out just three aspects that make a worship service by God's design ordinary. Biblical worship is limited, marked by routine, and above all simple.

Limited

The true Christian worship service has boundaries. In other words, we are not permitted to do—and therefore shouldn't do—whatever we want. The Bible regulates what goes on during a worship service. Lest we store up for ourselves the same kind of wrath experienced by Nadab and Abihu (Leviticus 10), we should take this seriously. There are many things that we could dream up to do in worship that would make it more exciting, more inviting to certain groups of people, and even more entertaining for us, but there are divinely set limitations. The biblical model for worship in God's house is not "Let all things be done," and certainly not "Let anything be done," but rather, "Let all things be done decently and in order" (1 Cor. 14:40).

Especially in an American context, it's hard to imagine how limits can be a good thing. We love excess. The consumerist impulse that drives our decision on Black Friday or Cyber Monday is often present on Sunday at church: we want the next coolest, sleekest, and boldest thing—and a lot of it too! Yet a careful examination of this way of life will show that it is unsustainable. "A default, normal, unexamined American life" is "exhausting," Justin Whitmel Earley correctly notes.[3] The limits God gives us—not only in all of life through His law but also in worship—are really meant for our good.

Earley writes that "when we act out the 'no-limits-none-ever' freedom liturgy, we assume that the good life comes from having the freedom to do whatever we want. So to ensure the good life, we have to ensure our ability to choose in each moment. But what if the good life doesn't come from having the ability to do what we want but

3. Earley, *Common Rule*, 23.

from having the ability to do what we were made for? What if true freedom comes from choosing the right limitations, not avoiding all limitations?"[4] It takes faith to believe that. It takes faith to receive these divinely appointed limitations with joy and to approach something as ordinary as Christian worship with anticipation and excitement, not dread or drudgery.

Routine

I brush my teeth every morning. I suppose there's nothing very exciting to report there. It's part of my daily routine (as I hope it is for you too). "Routine" is about the epitome of ordinary, isn't it? But that's exactly what worship is meant to be as well: routine. We go grocery shopping on Mondays, drive our kids to soccer on Wednesdays, have dinner at our in-laws on Thursdays, do household chores on Saturdays, and go to church on Sundays. And we do it all over again each week. There's nothing particularly remarkable about it. Sunday worship is meant to be a part of the warp and woof of our lives.

Maybe it wouldn't all sound so horrible if we replaced the word *routine* with *rhythm*—they are essentially the same thing, but the latter has a slightly more inviting ring to it. Worship is part of the rhythm that God wove into creation. It's the rhythm of stop and go, yes and no, work and rest. From the beginning the rhythm that we needed was six days in the world working and a day of coming back to God and worshiping and resting. That rhythm is still there and is still needed. The seasons provide needed rest for plants and vegetation to grow stronger and multiply the next year, just as we need that weekly rest so that our bodies can recover and our souls can grow. Faithful attendance in weekly worship and returning to God is part of flowing with that rhythm rather than fighting it. Adam and Eve ran and hid from God and disrupted the pattern that was established for their good—let's not make the same mistake.

Michael Horton helps reorient our thinking: "The Lord's Day is not another treadmill but a day of resting from our works as we bask in

---

4. Earley, *Common Rule*, 10.

[God's] marvelous provision for our salvation and temporal needs."[5] We must go to Him, run to and not from Him, and find in Him the rest our restless hearts so desperately need. Do you see it as such? Or is it a burden and a bore to you?

Beyond the weekly rhythm of Sunday church attendance, there's also the liturgical rhythm that we have seen takes place in the actual worship service. Every week we go to church, but beyond that we go to church expecting in many ways to experience the very same things we experienced the week before. We come because God calls us; we are drawn by this call to confess our sins before His inestimable holiness; we are reminded of the forgiveness that we have in Christ and that we belong to God through the proclamation of His word; we experience communion and fellowship with a reconciling God; and then we are commissioned back into the world to be His ambassadors of reconciliation. We tell the same gospel story every week, go through that same gospel logic every service, because it's what our hearts and minds so desperately need. The trajectory of this service will set the trajectory for the whole week—one of hope, confidence, and joy in Christ. As we understand this, we see that the routine and rhythm of worship is a blessing (1 Cor. 14:33).

Simple

D. G. Hart writes that "worship in the age of the Holy Spirit is not flashy or visibly powerful but instead is so simple that it appears to be inconsequential."[6] As we have seen in this book, that is the great problem most of mainstream Christianity has with corporate worship. The traditionally Reformed approach seems so simple that surely something must change. The two main ways to address this are either to make worship far more exciting and entertaining or to make worship far more ethereal and mystical. At least then the act of worship will seem to be significant.

What are these simple and seemingly inconsequential means of worship that are spurned by many Christians today? The word, the

---

5. Horton, *Ordinary*, 199.
6. Hart, *Recovering Mother Kirk*, 98.

sacraments, and prayer, all experienced corporately in the life of the church. They are often referred to as the ordinary (there's that word again) means of grace. Why "ordinary"? There is certainly nothing about the Scriptures that would attract itself to a modern society that has all but given up on reading. What could a book possibly do to give me a spiritual experience? Similarly, what is so spectacular about bread, wine, and water? The elements of the sacraments are culled from mundane, everyday life. "I can get those things at home," one might object, "so what makes church so special?" And prayer is certainly far from fantastical. Haven't we all, in our weakest moments, viewed it as a tedious chore?

And yet these elements are to fill the worship service because they are ordained by God to communicate His grace and blessing to us. The early church understood this: "And they continued steadfastly in the apostles' doctrine and fellowship, in the breaking of bread, and in prayers" (Acts 2:42). Do we? Are we content to persist in and dedicate ourselves to these simple means? We must remember that while they appear simple to the naked eye, the eye of faith will see in them so much more.

Extraordinary

It is the Spirit who uses such ordinary things to bring about such marvelous ends. "But God has chosen the foolish things of the world to put to shame the wise, and God has chosen the weak things of the world to put to shame the things which are mighty" (1 Cor. 1:27). The Holy Spirit can make things that are seemingly ordinary to be of extraordinary significance for those who participate by faith. Are you participating by faith? Are you aware of what is really going on, what is really happening, when we worship? To prevent us from forgetting, I have sought to capture in summary form some of what has been said elsewhere in this book.

Dear worshiper, keep in mind the following three facts about worship to guard yourself from the fear of the Same Old Thing.

A Transformational Experience

I have emphasized throughout this volume that a supernatural aspect of worship is that it is transformative. God uses those simple means mentioned above (word, sacraments, and prayer) for extraordinary purposes—namely, sanctification. In fact, corporate worship is the primary arena of sanctification in the Christian life. In church we receive the ordinary means "whereby Christ communicates to us the benefits of redemption" (WSC 88). Worship is the garden where we best grow in grace, and these ordinary means water and nourish us in that growth. Here the old man is put to death and the new man is brought to life and cultivated. Herein lies yet another reason why church is not optional but truly vital for the Christian: it's how we become like Christ.

When I step out of the barber shop, it is expected that I will look different from when I stepped in—and not just different but preferably better! If twenty dollars and a half hour later I look exactly the same, my wife would rightly conclude that I am wasting my time and should go somewhere else. We should expect to "look" different coming out of church than when we first went in because in worship we are undergoing a transformation by God's Spirit.

Let me qualify that statement a bit. This difference is not a physical one, so it will not be perceptible to the eye. It takes place in the soul. And even that change is so small and incremental that it may not be readily apparent to those close to us—or even to ourselves for that matter! But for the Christian who comes to worship in faith, there is a change happening, and it will be noticeable—sooner or later. God's will for us is that we will change, that we will be transformed, that we will be sanctified (1 Thess. 4:3). We will look different coming out of a life of worship than when we first came in—and not just different, but better. Doesn't that make you want to go to church?

A Trinitarian Encounter

At the heart of the supernatural wonder of worship is that in worship we come before a supernatural being. As we have learned, in worship we meet with God by His sweet invitation. And this is precisely how we are transformed. Those moments where we might have a brief encounter with a celebrity are often indelibly imprinted on our minds: maybe the time we bumped into a world-class athlete or when we got to shake the hand of the president of the United States on his university tour. We tell those stories over and over since they seem to us to be once-in-a-lifetime events. But the Christian has something so much greater. We come before God Himself, not by chance but by His intentional invitation week after week. We have a standing meeting with the living God, the Creator of all things and the Redeemer of the elect.

Nor do we meet with God as an abstract being but rather as He reveals Himself to us in Scripture: a tripersonal God. Worship is inherently Trinitarian—it is "the communion of the holy Trinity with us his people," says theologian Robert Letham.[7] Our worship is directed to God the Father through the one Mediator between God and man, the Lord Jesus Christ, and by the power of the indwelling Holy Spirit. Corporate worship is a place where we come to know and experience each member of the Trinity. We come to know the love of the Father, lavished on us in the grace of the Son, experienced by the fellowship of the Holy Spirit (2 Cor. 13:14).

An Undeserved and Astounding Privilege

Perhaps the ultimate wonder of worship is that ordinary people like us could possibly give glory to such an extraordinary God. And this is the real reason we go to worship, after all. It is not primarily for what we can get out of it; that is a blessed consequence. Rather, it is for what we give God: the glory that is due His name (Ps. 29:2).

Isn't that a breathtaking thought? The God of the universe has appointed us to magnify Him, to praise Him, to exult in Him. Yes, the holy angels worship Him night and day. Yes, even all creation is a proof and proclamation of His grandeur. But God does not seek out their worship. He seeks out ours (John 4:23). The rocks could cry out if He wanted them to, but He doesn't want them to. He wants to hear our cry. And He is so desirous of our worship that He sent His Son to redeem us and enable us to give it to Him. All God's saving acts redound to His praise and glory. There is nothing more extraordinary than this.

---

7. Letham, "Trinity in Worship," in *Essential Trinity*, ed. Crowe and Trueman, 273.

Do you sense the privilege that is yours when you come to worship? Worship begins, as we have seen, with a call. Throughout the Scriptures we learn that when God calls people to a task, though it might be intimidating and weighty, it is ultimately a high privilege. It is a sign of His discriminatory favor: He has chosen this particular person (or people) to a special work, and no one else. Consider the response of the great prophets Isaiah and Jeremiah when God called them to minister to His people. Each responded with humbled disbelief. They recognized they were not worthy or deserving of the privilege that God was placing before them. Though they each had flaws and shortcomings, God promised to be with them and use them—they got to be vessels of His glory to the rest of the world. Similarly, the apostle Paul recognized that though he was the least of the saints (Eph. 3:8) and the chief of sinners (1 Tim. 1:15), God appointed and called him to apostleship in order that God would receive all "honor and glory forever and ever" (1 Tim. 1:17). Perhaps the best example is Mary, whose humble astonishment exuded in praise:

> My soul magnifies the Lord,
> And my spirit has rejoiced in God my Savior.
> For He has regarded the lowly state of His maidservant;
> For behold, henceforth all generations will call me blessed.
>   (Luke 1:46–48)

Mary recognized that she was of low estate. There was nothing about her that would suggest she should have been chosen by God or given a special status, yet even so, God set His affection on her and privileged her beyond measure.

Certainly we are not called by God to the same sort of redemptive purposes that the prophets, Paul, or Mary were called to. Nevertheless, we are called by God—every week, in fact. When we hear the call to worship, let it be a reminder to us that we have an undeserved and astounding privilege. We get to be the instruments and beacons of God's glory in this world. God wants to use us! Like Mary, there is nothing inherent within us to commend us to such a weighty task. We are as ordinary as they come. But this is where we see God using the ordinary for extraordinary purposes. Here the weak become strong and the poor become rich. Whatever your vocation in life, whatever your social status or pedigree, whatever your personal achievements and accomplishments, nothing can surpass the honor of being appointed to praise the God of the universe. What purpose and privilege God gives us. It should tune our hearts to sing with Mary, "My soul magnifies the Lord."

Discussion Questions
1. Why is *ordinary* such a despised term and concept in today's culture?

2. Generally, how are limitations actually good for us? How does this particularly apply to worship?

3. What is the importance of the rhythm of the Sabbath?

4. In what ways do we meet all three persons of the Godhead in corporate worship?

5. Describe the privilege that is ours to worship God.

Chapter 15

Preparing for, Participating in, and Profiting from Worship

Attention of body, intention of mind, and retention of memory are indispensably desired of all wisdom's scholars.
—John Trapp

I remember back in my senior year of college having a pretty easy class scheduled for Friday mornings. Early Friday mornings, that is, and I was not and am not a morning person. I would set the alarm for about ten minutes before the start of class, roll out of bed, brush my teeth, hop on my bike, and be sitting in the back row on time. And I wasn't just there on time; I was able to participate in class and do well with my grades. Like I said, it was a fairly easy course. It took almost no preparation whatsoever.

Worship isn't like that.

Worship is not the kind of thing that you can just roll out of bed and be ready for. Meeting with God is such a momentous event that it takes careful and sincere preparation. God Himself tells us that He expects us to prepare to meet with Him. If we think back to Mount Sinai, right before God made His first sustained appearance to old covenant worshipers, He instructed the people to come near the mountain, but not to enter His presence until they were prepared: "Then the LORD said to Moses, 'Go to the people and consecrate them today and tomorrow, and let them wash their clothes. And let them be ready for the third day. For on the third day the LORD will come down upon Mount Sinai in the sight of all the people'" (Ex. 19:10–11).

Israel was to prepare for three days before they met with their Maker and Redeemer! What kind of preparation do we afford God? Maybe we give Him only three minutes while the prelude is playing on Sunday morning. That is certainly important to do. Many churches helpfully remind people to "prepare their hearts" during a time of meditative music or silence before worship properly begins, perhaps additionally providing a pertinent verse of Scripture to reflect on. But if that is the extent of our preparation, then we will not be fully ready to meet with God. We can—and should—do more.

The Westminster Confession says that properly keeping the Sabbath entails, in part, the preparation of our hearts and the ordering of our common affairs beforehand (WCF 21.8). So what kinds of things can we do beforehand to ready our souls to meet with our great God and Savior? Since we have established that worship is comprised of both the ordinary and the extraordinary, it follows that our preparation will involve both simple, ordinary practices as well as challenging, soul-stretching, extraordinary ones.

"Ordinary" Practices

There are a number of simple things we can do in the days and moments leading up to worship to best prepare us to meet with God. There are even things we can be doing during and after the service to ensure a richer experience in worship. Preparing will lead to richer participation during and fruitful spiritual profiting afterward.[1] I list below some that have benefited my family and me over the years. These are practices we aim to keep. We sometimes fail, and you will too. But I can promise this: all the suggested practices for Lord's Day preparation are simple and achievable. And I think you'll find your soul enriched as you seek to implement them.

Don't Stay Out or Up Late on Saturday Night

Start here: on Saturday night, be a boring homebody. My suggestion is to stay in and go to bed early. I know that may sound difficult for some people, as many fun things happen on Saturday night. To your

---

1. For an extended resource on how to best participate in a worship service, Joel Beeke's *The Family at Church* (Grand Rapids: Reformation Heritage Books, 2008) is commended.

non-Christian friends, however, declining invitations to late-night get-togethers because you have church the next day will be a peculiar and therefore powerful witness. I recognize that "early" will mean different things for different people, and the amount of sleep we need to feel well rested varies from person to person, so use your best judgment in applying this principle.

We want to be wary of droopy eyelids in the worship service. A late night with friends does not aid in waking up on time the next day, ready and alert for what God has in store for you. Puritan Thomas Watson urged worshipers centuries ago to "take heed of drowsiness in hearing; drowsiness shows much irreverence. How lively are many when they are about the world, but in the worship of God how drowsy.... In the preaching of the Word, is not the bread of life broken to you; and will a man fall asleep at his food?"[2] Get a good night's rest before the Lord's Day. Our weak flesh doesn't need many excuses to catch some extra *z*'s during worship. Coming into the Lord's house alert and well rested will allow no foothold for the devil.

Don't Be Rushed Sunday Morning

We've all been there. Maybe something unexpected happened, like the new puppy went to the bathroom on the carpet right before you stepped out the door, or you get the whole family in the vehicle only to learn that the subzero overnight temperatures have killed the battery. Some things we can't avoid, but others we can. For instance, save needless hemming and hawing in front of the closet mirror on Sunday by deciding what to wear Saturday. Lay out your clothes the night before. That's all my wife and I do, and we leave the rest of our wardrobe preparation for the morning. But if you know you need to iron a shirt or dress, you could do that Saturday night as well. My grandfather would shine all his children's shoes Saturday night and meticulously line them up for ready use the next morning. If you have a lot of kids and mornings are inevitably hectic (okay, even one kid can do that), go the extra mile by setting up breakfast the night before. Seriously. Place the bowls

---

2. As quoted in I. D. E. Thomas, ed., *A Puritan Golden Treasury* (Edinburgh: Banner of Truth, 1977), 315.

and spoons around the respective seats at the table and set the boxes of cereal in the center for the family to swoop in and choose from.

Also, if you are serving in a particular way on Sunday (such as bringing snacks or teaching Sunday school), make sure you give yourself extra time for the preparation needed for that responsibility. We have a dear congregant who readies the coffee for our church practically every Sunday, and in order to prepare both for this service and her own soul on a given Sunday morning, she comes in each Saturday to get things set up beforehand. That is quite a commitment not only to serve each Sunday but also sacrifice a portion of her Saturday to do so. But the lesson we can learn is the importance of preparedness. Anything you can do to avoid the pressure, panic, and frustration of a rushed preparation for church should be done.

Cultivate a Good Attitude

If hustle and bustle is our norm on Sundays, then short tempers and emotional outbursts of some kind or another are almost inevitable. Hopefully following the aforementioned steps will help prevent that. But more than prevent a bad attitude on Sundays, we want to combat a bad attitude. That is, we should go on the offensive by intentionally striving to have a good, even joyful demeanor as we get ready and head off to church. We are going to do the most important thing on earth. How could we not be filled with anything but eager anticipation? To this end, Pastor Jason Helopoulos writes, "Cultivate a spirit of joy on Sunday mornings in your home. If this is the highlight of our week, then let's act like it. Talk about how wonderful the day is going to be, wake the kids up with excitement, turn on good Christian music for the whole family to listen to, and put a smile on your face."[3]

I have fond memories of the way my dad did exactly this when we were growing up. Every Sunday morning I awoke to the sound of Christian music playing from the living room entertainment center or sometimes from his upstairs office computer. He played songs we loved

---

3. Jason Helopoulos, "Preparing for Sunday Worship," *DeYoung, Restless, and Reformed* (blog), October 30, 2014, The Gospel Coalition, https://www.thegospelcoalition.org/blogs/kevin-deyoung/preparing-for-sunday-worship/.

as a family and that immediately brought a joyful spirit to our home. The standard weekday "just five more minutes!" for more sleep was cut off at the pass. For your home it might not be music, but consider what practices you might be able to implement that remind you and your family that this day is not only unique but also wonderful. The psalmist cries out, "I was glad when they said to me, 'Let us go into the house of the LORD'" (122:1). Does that ring true for you?

Review for Sunday

Many churches provide their order of worship online in the days leading up to the service or perhaps email a copy of the bulletin to the members of the church. On Saturday, why not review what will be coming up the next day? Read through the passage that will be preached and familiarize yourself with the text—even do some background reading if you wish![4] Also, see what hymns and psalms are being sung on Sunday. If you don't know one of them, read through it at home and practice singing it. Sadly—especially with music—sometimes we can be distracted by the "newness" of things. This is one way of preventing that kind of distraction on Sunday when our focus should be on God. So if at all possible, do some review before you get to church and don't be caught off guard by what goes on in the service. Unfamiliarity is quite good at breeding contempt.

Learn to Linger

We have seen from Acts 2:42 that the early church not only devoted themselves to preaching, praying, and the sacraments but also to the fellowship of the saints. Sunday is a day for community: the community of faith. It can be easy to attend church much like one might attend the movies. We grab our seats and scroll through our phones or chat with our buddies while we wait for the service to begin and sit dutifully during the "show," but then once we hear the benediction (the cinematic

---

4. Even if you are unable to access your church's order of worship before Sunday morning, you should at least have some idea what the sermon will be on if the pastor is preaching through a book of the Bible.

equivalent of rolling credits), we gather our things and head straight for the car.

If this looks something like your average Sunday, then, dear friend, your experience of the blessing of God's day and God's people is lamentably incomplete. We have already talked about the importance of getting to church on time. In addition to that, staying just a few minutes after the service could be the simple change that will revolutionize your churchgoing experience, says Pastor Whitney Clayton. In his experience, the people who regularly put this into practice make stronger friendships and inevitably find ways to serve.[5] So don't zip on home immediately after the service. Stick around and love your neighbors by asking about their lives. Get to know the community of faith in which God has placed you. Look outside of yourself and your situation by finding ways to serve. Prepare for Sunday by readying yourself, your family, and your schedule to hang around a few minutes afterward.

"Extraordinary" Preparation

Some aspects of preparing for worship are more spiritually weighty than those mentioned above. This does not mean they are any less achievable, but they are practices that recognize the extraordinary and supernatural exercise you are about to undertake. With the Spirit's help, you can implement these as well for the good of you and your family and especially for the glory of the God you worship.

Honor the Sabbath

It has been called the forgotten commandment of today (it's the fourth of ten, by the way). "Observe the Sabbath day, to keep it holy, as the LORD your God commanded you" (Deut. 5:12). Debates continue over what it means to properly observe the Sabbath day, and we will not be entering into them in this book.[6] Suffice it to say that we have certainly

---

5. Whitney Clayton, "The Small Change That Can Radically Improve Your Church Experience," *Facts & Trends*, July 18, 2018, https://factsandtrends.net/2018/07/18/the-small-change-that-can-radically-improve-your-church-experience/?fbclid=IwAR3wk_KpojQPxCG17vycBrUifU7N32-sLkekmpylE8a9P-JdYXXNnnGDp7s.

6. For further study on this subject, I recommend Joseph A. Pipa Jr., *The Lord's Day* (Fearn, Rosshire, Scotland: Christian Focus, 2013); and Walter Chantry, *Call the Sabbath*

failed at preparing to meet with God if we have not even carved out the time to meet with Him. He has hallowed this one day in seven, and He desires that we hallow it in our lives as well.

In my observation, work and youth sports are two of the most common threats to sanctifying Sunday and the time we have to worship God.[7] We try to make church meet our needs and fit our schedule. If we have to drive our kids to a soccer tournament, then we simply go to the early service or listen to a sermon on the way there, or, more often than not, we just miss worship entirely. When we miss out on worship, we miss the banquet that God has set for our starving and thirsting souls. We don't want that for ourselves, and certainly not for our families. So we see that worship and Sabbath observance go hand in hand. Let us not neglect to meet together on God's day to do His bidding, as sadly is the habit of some (Heb. 10:25).

But it's hard. There are so many things that compete and clamor for our attention and time, and many of them seem like good things. It can be really difficult to say no. The sooner we cultivate this biblically mandated practice of keeping the Lord's Day holy, the better it will be. In my estimation, the fact that God has set aside every Sunday in its entirety makes it easier to say no to certain things and guard my schedule. I never need to question what I might be doing that particular Sunday since God has told me in His word what to do: I am to worship and rest. It's the idea of freedom within limitations. I have freedom to worship God and say no to other activities because this is the limitation that He has placed on His creatures—and what a grand limitation it is!

We need to recognize we're not being rude to those around us when we decline to participate in worldly activities for the sake of heavenly ones. Why not? In one sense, it's as simple as the truth that God made the appointment with us first. You've certainly had that frustration of trying to schedule a lunch with a friend. Perhaps the two of you have pulled out your phones and are comparing schedules:

---

a Delight (Edinburgh: Banner of Truth, 2000). The latter has a bibliography of other helpful titles on this important topic.

7. A few friends suggest other common threats: fishing/hunting, golf, extra sleep, and "family time"—apparently for some, worship isn't considered quality time with family.

"How about Wednesday lunch?"

"Sorry. Can't. I have a doctor's appointment. But Friday works."

"Nope. No good for me. The in-laws are in town."

It's not considered rude when you can't make something work because of a prior engagement. Likewise, our response to the world regarding Sunday activities that draw us away from concerted, uninterrupted worship is that we have a scheduling conflict. "No," we must say. "I can't make that work. I have an appointment with God."

Properly preparing for the Sabbath will mean properly thinking about the Sabbath. It is not a burden or a chore. It is something that we are to call a delight (Isa. 58:13)! It is a gift; hence, God says we were not made for the Sabbath, to bow down to it in slavish dread and exasperation, but it was made for us. The Sabbath is a wonderful provision from God to remind us every week that the way to Him is through the gospel and rest, not through the law and works. Horton explains, "It is the opportunity to receive a kingdom rather than to build one; to be beneficiaries rather than benefactors; to be heirs rather than employees."[8]

I certainly want that. In fact, I need that, and so do you. In knowing we need it, we will be more likely to apprehend it. So seek to have a proper, biblical conception of what the Sabbath is. The Sabbath reminds us we belong to God and not this passing world. It reminds us we are more than conquerors and cannot be defeated. It reminds us that Christ is King, and He has secured eternal peace for His people. It's not about sitting quietly in a dim living room, going mad with boredom. And while it is about saying no to certain things that we might like, it is also about saying yes to things that are far better: "Setting aside the ordinary callings and pastimes of the week, our calling on the Lord's Day is to share, together with our coheirs, in the powers of the age to come. It is not by simply *emptying* the day with a list of rules, but by *filling* it with treasure hunting, that the Christian Sabbath orients us, our families, and our fellow saints to our heavenly citizenship."[9]

---

8. Horton, *Ordinary*, 199.

9. Horton, *Ordinary*, 176, emphasis original.

Pray

We should always be in prayer, but Saturday evening and Sunday morning would be particularly good times to spend in earnest prayer before our Lord. The world, the flesh, and the devil are always clamoring for our affections and attention, and perhaps never more viciously than on the Lord's Day. According to C. S. Lewis's Screwtape, a primary task of devils is to distract people from the present and from eternity. In Christian worship, eternity enters into the present, so you can be sure devils will be at work with distraction. There will be innumerable excuses popping into our heads to keep us from church. We are too tired, too busy, too introverted, too whatever. Then when we are there we will also face an onslaught of distractions. Funny how carpet patterns never seem so interesting as when an earnest preacher sets out to exposit a perceived tedious passage of Scripture. Drifting eyes are a sign of a restless and wandering heart and are equivalent to sleeping with the eyes open.

So what is a person to do? Pray. And pray for what exactly? Here are just a few suggestions. Pray that God would give you the proper desire to worship Him and serve Him with His people. Pray that the Spirit would open your heart to be challenged and changed by the preached word. Ask that your thoughts would be kept captive to Christ and the cares of the week past or the worries of the week ahead would not distract you (or things like carpet patterns, either!). Pray for those who will be leading the service in music, prayers, and Scripture reading. Pray for your pastor and for his sermon preparation and delivery. Pray that unbelievers would enter through the doors and come to saving faith. Above all, pray that Christ would be exalted, magnified, and glorified among His people.

Get Right with Your Fellow Worshipers

Did you know that at one point in the Sermon on the Mount Jesus takes up the topic of worship? It's actually tucked into His teaching on anger. He says, "Therefore if you bring your gift to the altar, and there remember that your brother has something against you, leave your gift there before the altar, and go your way. First be reconciled to your brother, and then come and offer your gift" (Matt. 5:23–24).

The language of bringing an offering to an altar places us in the setting of worship, as Jesus drew on the practice of temple worship that was still in effect during His lifetime. Jesus offered this as an example and practical application of the principles He had just set forth regarding anger. The illustration includes two believers (hence, the use of "brother") who are at odds with one another. According to the teaching of our Savior, this kind of anger, conflict, and division among believers is not acceptable in the place of worship. The command is to make things right with the offended brother and then come to worship, the implication being that the "gift"—the worship—would otherwise be sullied and not acceptable before God.

Why is this? Why is reconciliation between fellow worshipers such an important part of preparation for worship? It's because worship is all about reconciliation. As we have seen throughout this book, corporate worship is when Christians can experience the reconciliatory heart of God and the reconciliatory power of the gospel. Sin alienates us from God—it got us kicked out of the garden and cast away from God's presence. And yet God sent His Son to bring us back home to Him. Though we will experience that fellowship with God perfectly and everlastingly in heaven, we get a taste of it now. We get a picture of what it looks like to be reconciled to God every Sunday: we are invited to His house, we are encouraged to come before His feet for prayer and instruction, and we are seated around His table to feast on His grace.

Paul tells us that a major reason we have been reconciled to God is so that we would be reconciled to one another (2 Cor. 5:18). Since God has forgiven us our many sins, we can forgive others for whatever sins they may commit against us, and we can have the humility to ask for forgiveness whenever we have done wrong against them. And perhaps we would do better if we realized that this issue cannot be separated from worship. We prove that we really have not understood the reconciliation we have received from God if we refuse to be reconciled to our brothers and sisters in Christ. It is hypocritical to enter church on Sunday, into the very house of reconciliation, if we are harboring anger or resentment or bitterness toward others who have been welcomed to that house.

As we touched on in a previous chapter, properly participating in the Lord's Supper will entail this outward-facing, horizontal love and reconciliation with our fellow worshipers. Acts tells us that the early church grew and flourished as the saints met for worship and the sacrament "with gladness and singleness of heart, praising God, and having favour with all the people" (Acts 2:46–47 KJV). Paul condemns those Corinthians who came to the table while there was division in the church (1 Cor. 11:18). It is fitting, then, that the Westminster divines instruct us to prepare for the Lord's Supper by examining our "love to God and the brethren" and by "forgiving those that have done [us] wrong" (WLC 171). This is the necessary way to approach not only the Supper but all of worship.

Get Right with God

The most important aspect of preparing for worship is also the most obvious, but it must be stated nonetheless: we need to have a proper relationship with the One we worship. If we are coming as enemies of God, as slaves to sin and not as servants of the Most High, the whole endeavor is in vain. You can be a churchgoer your whole life, but if you have not received Jesus Christ in faith then it will be for nothing. Undoubtedly on the last day there will be many who will fall before the judgment throne of Christ crying out, "Lord, Lord, did we not regularly attend Your worship services? Did we not often come early to set up and stay late to tear down? Did we not sing in the choir and serve in the kitchen and help in the nursery? Did we not labor in Your church as elders, deacons, trustees, accountants, secretaries, custodians? Did we not bow our heads when we were told to pray and stand when we were told to sing and listen when the pastor preached?" And to this Jesus will reply, "I did not know you" (see Matt. 7:21–23).

You need to know God—or rather be known by God (as Paul says, cf. Gal. 2:20)—to really worship in spirit and in truth. You need to know yourself as a sinner in need of saving and believe the good news of a substitute Savior who came into the world for sinners. We need to be right with God by having the righteousness of Christ covering our sin as we enter His holy presence. Receiving that message in faith and repentance prepares us each Lord's Day to meet with God not as a judge but as a loving Father.

Of course, the elements of the worship service that we have studied are the very things often used by the Spirit to bring about that faith and repentance. In worship we learn of our sinful condition and of our spiritual plight. But in worship the gospel is also proclaimed, and the saving power, mercy, and love of Jesus Christ are offered freely to all who will take of them. In other words, God uses worship to make worshipers. Hearts of stone are melted under the simple ordinary means of preaching, sacraments, and prayer, and new hearts that beat for God are formed in their place. This is the Spirit's doing. For our part, though, we must come ready to receive what God has for us. If you do not know Christ in a saving way, when you enter into a church service be ready to receive what is offered to you there—it could just be that the Holy Spirit will change your heart.

Once God becomes your God you will truly worship Him. Knowing Him through faith in Jesus Christ is the preparation needed for right and reverent worship. That's where it begins. That is the start of it all—and it's the end of it all as well, which is why I conclude with this exhortation. Your love for worship will grow in proportion to your love for your God and Savior; once you see all that He has done for you, all that He has given to you, all that He has lavished on you, you are His and He is yours. My prayer is that the words of Isaiah 25:1 would capture what it is you do on Sundays—and why you do it:

> O LORD, You are my God.
> I will exalt You,
> I will praise Your name,
> For You have done wonderful things.

Is God your God? Have you come to know and believe and experience the things He has done in the gospel? If so, exaltation and praise are the only fitting response. The "wonderful things" of God demand a life—and even more specifically a worship—that is full of wonder, love, and praise.

Conclusion

In many respects, the entire aim of this book has been to prepare you for worship. It is my conviction that the best way to prepare for worship is identical to the best way to participate in and profit from worship, and that is to know what is happening.

When we worship God, we are drawn by His Holy Spirit into His very presence to have a personal encounter with Him. What would otherwise be a terrifying thought becomes a joyful experience as we learn that we are covered in the perfection of Jesus Christ and fully accepted in the Beloved. We come before God not on our own but with the body of believers whom we have been spiritually united to. There is strength in numbers, and these numbers are ultimately not seen by how many bodies are in the pews but by the innumerable multitude around the world and in the heavenly places whom we join with in worship.

In worship God confirms to us that we are doing the most important thing, and this gives us joy and purpose. It begins fittingly with a call from God since we are most satisfied when we are submitting to our Maker and doing His bidding. Throughout the service, as we are reminded of and reprimanded for our sins, we are also offered gospel hope. We learn that we do not belong to our sin, but to God's Son. This is further confirmed as God consecrates us as His own through the preaching of His sacred and sanctifying word and then communes with us as His dear children around His Table.

From start to finish the service impresses on us our true identity. We receive the indelible name that God gives us, not the false and fragile names that the world has offered in the preceding week. And now, confident of our status before Him, emboldened through the justification we have in the Son, and empowered by the indwelling Holy Spirit, we go. We are equipped to face the hardships of a world of sin because of the superabundant grace that God has poured out on us. We go out with a mission: to be God's emissaries and shine light in a dark world. Empowered by God's Spirit, we are called to find more worshipers.

Don't forget to bring them with you next week.

Discussion Questions

1. What are some Scripture passages that show us God wants us to prepare before we meet Him?

2. What are some of your own practices for preparing your heart to meet with God in worship?

3. What are some of the benefits of coming to church early and leaving late?

4. What is the connection between Sabbath and worship?

5. What does it mean to be right with fellow worshipers as well as with the One we worship? How are you doing at these things?